Forty Days to Fermenting Success:

**Build your fermenting flair, arouse your taste buds
and kick your gut into gear!**

Susan Pargman

Thanks be to…

My good friend and fellow fermenter April Myers
for her editing and encouragement.

Family friends, the Lamars,
who fermented their way through each recipe as tasters and testers.

Husband, Steve,
for proofing the pages
and eating everything I've ever made without complaining.

Mom, who has always been my biggest fan.

CONTENTS

INTRODUCTION – How to use this book

Forty Days to Fermenting Success is a gateway to building your creativity in the kitchen, enjoying new tastes and improving your health (digestive and otherwise).

This step-by-step tool will help you ease into the art of fermentation. You get to dabble with creating a variety of fermented dishes a little at a time.

First, you'll master one simple technique for converting an everyday grain into a delicious, healthful breakfast overnight. Then on subsequent days, you'll add new techniques to your culinary résumé involving vegetables, fruits and dairy.

I think that's how creativity works best. Get familiar with some techniques, and it will open the door to confidently creating and personalizing tasty dishes to share with the loved ones who join you at the table.

Forty Days to Fermenting Success is organized as a "one day at a time" food-making journey. But there's no need to keep to a rigid calendar schedule as you master different techniques and explore intriguing tastes.

Discover new ferments one section at a time, if you like. Try out the techniques, check out the tips and make your own notes as you go along. Or skip through to something else on the menu that tickles your personal taste buds. (And I've found that taste buds are quite ticklish!)

Got questions?

I figured you would have some by Day 23. That's where I've added in the most frequently asked questions. So go ahead and skip on over to Day 23 if you're wondering about something. I may have an answer for you!

Then on Day 37, just as you're wondering whether you REALLY have time to ferment, I've given you some handy hints on how to take a break from fermenting. You'll find ways to put your microbes on vacation so that you can take one too!

Fermenting for a new generation

Fermenting may seem like a mystery to some people because it's an art that's skipped a couple of generations in some families.

I never knew my great-grandmother, but back in Oklahoma, she kept a closet off the kitchen especially for fermenting all kinds of food. That was before refrigeration. At that time, fermenting your food was the safest way to preserve it – just as it still is today.

As 21st century men and women explore and discover the health benefits of the foods we pile on our plates, fermenting has re-joined the game as a major player in our gut health!

As you launch out to explore strange new worlds and seek out new probiotic life, I raise a glass of Superfood Sangria to you (find it on Day Thirty-Five)! Here's to:

- *new taste,*
- *new health,*
- *creative endeavors and*
- *a party every night!*

DAY ONE: Bacteria – healthy, toxic, or both?

On Day One of your *Forty Days to Fermenting Success* you'll start to build a foundation of knowledge about what fermenting is, and why it's worth a look.

On my "Day One," I didn't have a clue. Just a confounding mystery…

My family's multi-generational history of Crohn's disease, Irritable Bowel Syndrome, Colitis, Arthritis, Allergies and Celiac disease was that mystery. Trying to solve the mystery led me into a decades-long search for food-based solutions. We went gluten free. Lectin free. Dairy free. Nutrient dense. Vegan. Keto. And a lot of it helped some of us…. but some of it didn't help any of us.

It was clear that there was a piece missing from the puzzle. An itty-bitty, teensy weensy piece — or rather trillions of itty-bitty pieces.

In a word: bacteria — some types of which are especially associated with fermented foods. But wait —aren't we supposed to avoid bacteria? Isn't that what pasteurization and smearing gobs of anti-bacterial gel on our hands is all about?

Color me CONFUSED

To embrace (or at least give a friendly nod toward) bacterial fermentation as part of the journey to my family's health, I needed a serious paradigm shift. I had to get over the "all-bacteria-is-bad" hurdle. After all, you and I are filled to the gills with bacteria. And that's a good thing.

There are good bacteria (aka "gut buddies"), but there are also toxic bacteria (aka "gut baddies"). Here's my comic book version of how they work:

Toxin-producing bacteria, picked up through various environmental contaminations, slink through our innards poking holes through our happy places and sending invaders out into the rest of our body. They laugh maniacally while peering out from beneath pointy v-shaped eyebrows.

Enter our gut buddies – many of them that come to us through eating fermented foods. They're the super heroes who fly through our microbiome plugging up the holes, turning food into energy, fighting off infections and sending power up to our brain.

When you populate your gut with our little super-heroes by eating fermented foods, and they outnumber the toxic fellas maybe 8 to 1, they can stop trouble before you know it.

This is obviously a very simplified picture of our inner lives. But nothing about life is simple. Neither our innards nor our outards. Like… why the bacteria we consider harmful can actually come to the rescue at other times to chase off some of the worst toxin-producers. (E-coli vs. salmonella https://www.ocregister.com/2013/10/25/bacteria-battle-e-coli-helps-fight-salmonella/) What???

And why people that make us crazy in some ways can end up being our best buddies in other ways. What??? I remain confused. Life is fuzzy at best.

I eat you, you eat me

The paradigm shift tips even more aslant as I recognize that while I'm consuming a variety of microbes – they are consuming me. In a good way.

My gut buddies use the foods I eat to work on my behalf, improving my health, and leveling-up my life. With names like Bifidobacteria and Lactobacillus, they help manufacture bio-chemicals inside me that contribute to physical and mental health.

My job is to conscientiously feed them the right stuff to keep the active bacteria working, diversifying and defeating disease.

What to feed them… er… me? Fermented foods! That's because ferments such as those described in this book, contain live, healthy bacteria we depend on, plus the fiber that keeps the whole give-and-take system running.

Making friends with microbes

Creating fermented foods especially appealed to the "mad scientist" part of me when I found out that I could grow a community of good bacteria in a glass jar. Tucked away on a shelf. In my laundry room. Cheap.

Taking care of this little community of microbes-in-jars has become part of my regular rounds. "How ya smellin' little buddies? I see those bubbles! Good work!"

In this photo on the right, you see short bottles on the top shelf with a thermometer to help me monitor the temperature. I like it to be right around 70 degrees F. Center shelf is for the tall bottles of liquid ferments like water kefir, kombucha and apple cider vinegar. Down on the bottom are veggie ferments in a lasagna dish to catch spills. On the right is a little heater (the kind you might have under your desk to warm your feet) that I can adjust to help keep the temperature consistent in the winter.

I made a canvas cover to flap down over the front. That helps keep it dark for the ferments that like the dark. And it helps keep the temperature consistent. Because it's cotton canvas, it's breathable.

I'm not worried about cross-contamination of microbes jumping from one jar to the other. Most of the jars have a lid. I don't open the lids until I take the jars into the kitchen for tasting and re-bottling.

However, I have read about someone who had trouble when she cultured her sourdough starter next to cheese. The sourdough went rogue and the cheese puffed up like cumulus clouds over Tahiti.

Seems that sometimes various yeasts and bacteria don't get along. Sort of like the Hatfields and McCoys/ Yankees and Dodgers/ Letterman and Leno feuds all over again.

Do your best to keep the peace. Group similar ferments together if you can. But if you can't, don't sweat it. Armed with knowledge, you can be alert for signs of battling microbes.

Lacto-fermentation

The magic of changing fresh foods into delightful fermented dishes like pickles, kimchi, yogurt, kombucha and sauerkraut usually works through the process of lacto-fermentation. Veggies and fruits have lactobacillus on them naturally. Yogurt, kefir and kombucha need a starter added to them to get that process rolling.

Alcoholic fermentation

Wine and beer are some examples of food fermented with yeast, which transform sugar into alcohol as a byproduct.

These two types of fermentation aren't mutually exclusive, nor are they the only two kinds of fermentation there are. Some foods, like sourdough bread, are a combination of both. And vinegar is sour because it produces acetic acid, not lactic acid.

NOTE: The reason that fermented food tastes sour or tangy is because over time, the microbes feast on the sugars in your food, converting carbohydrates into alcohol and acids, and so remove much of the sweetness and leave their lactic acid signature flavors behind.

The magic of you

As the chief magician and bottle washer in your enchanted realm known as *"KIT-chen"*, you get the opportunity to decide on what you want to make, combine your chosen foods with some simple ingredients and enjoy the process… including washing the bottle, of course.

I'm not mad, just hungry

For the not-so-mad scientists, you can also buy good ferments made by reputable food companies. Just make sure they aren't canned, pasteurized or otherwise heated to death. You'll find them in the refrigerated section of your market. Look for "CONTAINS LIVE CULTURES" on the label.

Join a community of (human) fermenting friends

As you get comfortable with the idea of creating your own fermented foods, you'll find that the job gets easier if you can make some human friends, taste their ferments and trade ideas for developing new tastes and skills.

Check your local club listings to see if there's a fermenting group nearby. There's nothing in my region, so I combined joining a fermenter's club online with dragging some of my friends over to my house to learn together.

When several of my friends didn't come back after our massively messy sauerkraut escapades, I joined an unsuspecting local community help-group and forced… I mean… *invited* some of my new friends to come over and make fermented food and beverages with me.

As word gets around that you're that kooky neighbor with the ripe-smelling laundry room, fermented food lovers will show up on your lawn.

Happily, the ranks of the folks who enjoy fermenting aren't a pasteurized or even a homogenized social group. Just like the inner world of our gut buddies, we include all kinds, and that's good.

Most of my fermenting friends, both new and old are naturally inclined to share. We share SCOBYs (Symbiotic Culture Of Bacteria and Yeast), kefir grains, sourdough starters, recipes, experience (good and bad), or whatever else is needed to empower one another's success.

If some of these words are new to you, give yourself 39 more days, and you'll be chitchatting, using all kinds of new vocabulary without breaking a sweat!

Recommended reading

Since Day One is about getting familiar with the idea of intentionally breeding certain kinds of bacteria in a bottle, you can expand your knowledge with a trip to the library. Some books I've enjoyed include:

- *Fermentation on Wheels* by Tara Whitsitt (an exciting adventure of a young lady who rigged up a bus as a fermentation station and traveled across the USA and back.)
- *The Noma Guide to Fermentation* by Redzepi and Zilber (the Scandinavian restaurateurs who prepare gorgeous fermented foods foraged from local sources.)
- *The Art of Fermentation* by Sandor Ellix Katz (seriously the leading, beloved, laid-back self-taught fermentation expert of our day.)

If you're inclined to search the Internet for health information, look up articles researched and posted by reputable sources. Some suggestions include doing a search for:

- Harvard Health Fermented Foods.
- National Institutes of Health Fermented Foods.
- Tufts University Fermented Foods.

It's thrilling to think that our inner world is so busy and alive with gut buddies who exist to keep us charged up and moving forward every day. In *Forty Days to Fermenting Success* I hope to introduce you to what you need to start your journey to better health, including tools, hints for basic fermenting, a few recipes and lots of enthusiastic encouragement.

NOTE ON STARTING TO EAT FERMENTS:
Go slowly at first. Your gut bacteria population needs to transform just a little at a time, or you could experience some –ahem—"discomfort."

Your first ferment, one small bowl of fermented overnight oats as described on Day Two, should start you out on a gentle path. (Especially good if you slice a banana on top.)

Moving forward, a small forkful of fermented vegetables one day, a 2 ounce "gut shot" of sauerkraut juice another time, or ¼ cup of kvass with a meal is a good way to gauge the condition of your gut. Cut back if you have problems. Add a bit more if you find you're doing well. Over time, you'll balance your gut bacteria with more good guys than toxin-producers.

How much time? It took over half a year before our most sensitive family member could raise the flag of even a fragile victory. It did my heart good to hear her say, "Hey, I'm all out of sauerkraut. And while you're at it, can I try some beet kvass?"

Motor boat, motor boat
Go so slow...
motor boat, motor boat
Go so fast...
Motor boat motor boat
step on the gas!

DAY TWO: Wait for it… wait for it… Making your first ferment

On Day Two of your *Forty Days to Fermenting Success,* you'll make your first ferment – an overnight fermented bowl of oatmeal.

When you ferment a food, you cut and mix and squeeze and slosh things together. Then you bottle it up and wait, allowing those fruits, vegetables, grains and proteins to go through a natural metabolic process. When it's done, the nutrients will be more available, and the anti-nutrients will have been reduced.

They say that putting your ingredients together is the easiest part. It's the waiting that's hard! But that's what you've got to do. It takes time for your microscopic buddies to break the ingredients down into a simpler, more digestible food.

When the fermenting time is complete, your new food has a different flavor, tang and texture. Now it's filled with health-promoting probiotics that it didn't have before.

Whatcha' gonna make first?

Overnight Oats. You can put this nourishing bowl together tonight and have it for breakfast tomorrow morning. ALMOST instant gratification.

Tools you need:
- measuring cup
- measuring spoon
- bowl, pot or jar
- loose lid such as a cloth or paper coffee filter secured with rubber band
- spoon to stir the oats
- knife to chop toppings if desired

Ingredients (vary according to your own taste preference):

- 1 cup old-fashioned rolled oats
- 1 cup warm (non chlorinated) water
- 2 tablespoons of yogurt or milk kefir (with live cultures) as a "starter" for your ferment
- *If you don't want to use dairy,* you can use 1½ teaspoons of lemon juice or apple cider vinegar in its place as your "starter."

- a pinch of non-iodized salt

Process:

1. Put oats, water, yogurt (or other starter) and salt into a bowl, saucepan or jar and stir.
2. Cover with a cloth or paper coffee filter secured with a rubber band and leave at room temperature overnight.
3. In the morning, add water or milk as you like to soften the consistency.
4. Stir in some toppings, such as:
   - chopped almonds, pecans or walnuts
   - dried raisins, currants, apricots, figs, dates or other fruit
   - maple syrup, honey or brown sugar
   - cinnamon, butter, cream
   - bits of fresh bananas, peaches or apples

You can eat your finished bowl as-is, or warm it up for a few minutes before eating.

It's so nice to get up and have breakfast nearly ready to eat in the morning. If you like what you made, stir up a bigger batch next time. After fermenting your big batch overnight, keep the surplus fermented oats in your refrigerator to dip into the next day.

NOTE ABOUT STARTERS:

Starters are beneficial microorganisms that help get fermentation started. They have names like Lactobacillus plantarum, Streptococcus thermophilus, Kluyveromyces marxianus and other names that sound like they might be friends with Luke Skywalker.

Some foods benefit from adding a starter, but many can be fermented without anything but the bacteria already on the food and in the air.

What can be used as a starter? The whey you drain from an active-culture yogurt or milk kefir is often recommended. But it's not your only choice.

Brine from a previously fermented food like pickles or sauerkraut works. Also miso paste if it contains live cultures. I've never tried powdered, packaged cultures, so I can't personally recommend using them.

If using a starter, try to compliment the flavor of the starter with the food you want to ferment.

DAY THREE – Vinegar – attracts more flies than honey!

You just can't trust that old expression, "You can attract more flies with honey than with vinegar." Nope. Actually, flies are in the market for the microbes on fermenting fruit. So when they smell the acetic acid in vinegar, they'll swoop down on it.

Now you know why you need to cover your jar when you're making vinegar!

Why make vinegar?

The vinegar we're going to start to make on Day Three is apple cider vinegar (ACV). In the store, you'll buy a 32 oz bottle of raw organic ACV for around $8-$10. Making your own costs you six apples, a half-cup of sugar and a jar of water. Plus the wondrous ingredient of time.

Every spoonful of this stuff is full of beneficial bacteria. Plus it's useful in a variety of ways – even beyond attracting flies, if that's what you had in mind.

Some people drink a spoonful each day, diluted in water or juice, for their digestive health. You can also use it to give sparkling water a tangy taste. Or water it down to dab on itchy skin. It makes a nice astringent for your beautiful (or handsome) face. Dilute it to kill bacteria on kitchen surfaces, fruits and veggies. This stuff fights mold and mildew, soothes a sore throat and makes your hair shiny clean.

The real question is… why NOT make vinegar? Here's how to make a half-gallon.

Ingredients:

- around 6 organic apples, mixed sweet and tart for best flavor
- ½ cup sugar
- 1 tablespoon of raw, organic apple cider vinegar (optional)
- non-chlorinated water to fill the jar

Process:

1. Dissolve sugar in a cup of warm water and allow it to cool to room temperature.
2. Cut up apples into chunks. Keep the peels on the apples, as this is where the natural yeast resides that starts the ferment.
3. Fill a half-gallon sized WIDE MOUTH jar ¾ full with apple chunks.
4. Pour in cooled sugar water.

5. Fill the jar the rest of the way with cool water to within an inch of the top.
6. Optionally you can add a tablespoon of raw, organic apple cider vinegar "with the mother." But you don't have to do that.
7. Stir and cover with a breathable cloth (like calico cotton – not cheesecloth) or a paper coffee filter affixed with a rubber band. Remember, those flies are going to smell this and want some. Your breathable cover needs to firmly tell them to *buzz off!*
8. Set your jar on the counter top. Give your fermenting vinegar a stir each day with a non-metal object. It likes air, so you want to agitate the liquid a bit each day to share the air, and so that mold won't get a foothold.

As always… wait for it.

After one week, you can smell the apples. They're sending bubbles up to the top of your brew just to say, "I'm in here… I'm alive." After about two weeks when you see that the liquid has turned cloudy and a little bit darker, strain out the apples. Put the liquid back into your jar. Cover the jar again with a breathable cloth.

Continue to stir or swirl the liquid every day.

After another week, it may smell a little alcoholic and taste bitter. That's because vinegar goes through a couple of stages. First it converts the carbohydrates in the apples and sugar into alcohol.

Then it converts the alcohol into acetic acid, which gives vinegar its tanginess.

After several weeks, you will see a "mother of vinegar" (a ghostly swath of friendly bacteria) floating in your jar. Don't worry. It turns out that she's the VIP of the party. The living entity that turns your juice into vinegar.

After a total of six weeks, taste your ACV. Is it tangy yet? Has the bitterness mellowed? If not, let it go a little longer till it is. Maybe two months! Bottle your vinegar when it tastes right and store it at room temperature. It will not be as acidic as the vinegars you buy in the stores. That means you can't use it in canning, if that's something you do. But it WILL be delicious.

DAY FOUR – Setting up for the party
(Rated PG-13 for explicit content)

I hate to sound negative, but oxygen is not desirable in lactic acid fermentation of fruits and veggies. As the Primary Fermenting Coordinator (PFC), it's your job to create an environment (set up the party) that helps good bacteria thrive.

Under the juice, brine or other liquid, your lively little micro-friends meet up, dance, get married and make babies. They grow, eat, pass CO_2 gas and may even produce ethyl alcohol. Not unlike revelers at a New Year's Eve party in Times Square. Except in Times Square they've got air.

As the PFC in charge of the festivities, you'll set the mood and environment to give the micro-party-goers the best chance to mix and mingle.

They'll need a nice, clean ballroom – er – vessel. Like a crock or bowl or jar washed out with hot water, free of mold or crusty bits of past occupants.

The fruits and veggies you choose for your ferment should be nourishing and free from things that will put a damper on the fun: no pesticides, waxes, chemicals, mold or rot (ew!)

Use salt that's free from additives. Just say "no" to anti-caking compounds and added iodine. Iodine is a bacteria-killing agent. And speaking of bacteria killers, if you've got chlorine or other chemicals in your tap water it could end the party faster than Uncle Jesse whipping out his fascinating photos of the day he visited the world's largest ball of string. It happens. But chlorinated water should not happen. Spring water, filtered water or well water is way better to keep this party rolling.

No air allowed?

But what about that "no air allowed" sign hanging on the door? I mean, we're on planet earth, are we not? We're surrounded by oxygen, are we not?

Are these hard-partying bacteria really that delicate that they must live in some kind of a vacuum? I'll venture to say they aren't.

Then I'll venture to say maybe just a little bit delicate. They can be vulnerable to spoilage – especially if their surroundings have mold spores floating about. Just to be on the safe side, you may consider using some of the following:

- followers (things to hold the veggies under the brine)
- weights (things to hold the followers in place)
- lids (things to keep out mold, bugs and evaporation)

Followers

Say you get your fruit and veggies tamped tightly into the jar. *Good work!* Say you've got enough juice up to the top to cover it all. *High five!* Now say a few of your party-hardy food bits decide to float up and breach the surface, leaving them liable to dry out, attract mold spores, and miss out on the lacto-fermenting action. *(BUZZ!)*

That's where your follower comes in handy. A follower is something that you place on top of your fermenting foods to encourage them to stay below the brine.

Famous followers include slices of lemons. A leaf of cabbage. Pieces of unbleached muslin or parchment paper. Silicone cupcake baking cups. ViscoDisc canning buddies. Homemade food grade mesh or silicone cut to size and wedged into the jar just below the brine.

Weights

You may choose to use a weight if you think your follower might pop out of place. This could be a plate that fits down into your vessel. A food grade baggie with pie weights or marbles or gravel or brine sealed up inside. A glass disk. A smaller glass jar.

If you're certain your fermentation is firmly submerged using just a follower for the duration, great. The important thing here is keeping your fermenting food below the liquid using whatever works best for you.

Put a lid on it.

The less you expose your fermenting foods to oxygen, the less likely it is that you'll end up with unwelcome yeast and mold growing in there.

This is the type of lid that usually comes with your store-bought jars.

It's fine for canning purposes. But fermenting foods and salt water brine should not come into contact with metal for long periods of time. When you use a metal lid like this, leave plenty of headspace between the top of the brine and the lid.

While your food ferments, it generates carbon dioxide gas. As gas builds up, it creates a lot of pressure in the jar.

To prevent the pressure from warping your lid or breaking your jar, give the lid a little twist each day to relieve pressure. Open, (psst, gas escapes), close, done. Repeat each day while the fermenting food is letting off gas.

Here's an example of a one-piece waterless airlock lid with a built-in silicone valve. The one-way valve allows the gasses to passively escape. Gasses flow out, but oxygen can't get in.

You still need to keep an eye on your fermenting food to be sure it stays well under the liquid during the first part of the process. That's when certain bacteria are multiplying that need to be submerged to grow. After awhile, your food inside will re-absorb some of the liquid and you'll see the water level go down. Your food might look drier, but that's because it has absorbed the brine back into the food. That's nothing to worry over.

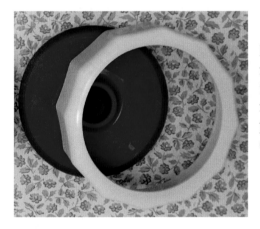

Here's a two-piece waterless airlock lid. The manufacturer sells the red piece, and you just pair it up with a jar ring bought from another manufacturer. It's a little flimsier than the one-piece lid above, but works the same and is easier on the budget.

The good old traditional ceramic water-seal crocks work well for fermenting veggies. Make sure the crock is not painted with lead-based paint. Crocks include a trough around the top that you fill with water. The lid fits down over that. The water seals the oxygen out, but allows gasses from inside to bubble through. They come in sizes anywhere from a half-gallon to 2 gallons and more.

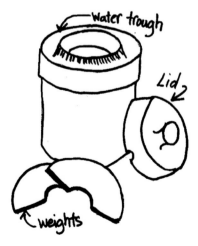

When your ferment is all done, you can remove the follower, change out the lid for a lid like this one and put it in the refrigerator. The cold temperature will slow down the fermenting process quite a bit. It won't stop altogether, but it will be slow enough that it probably won't need an airlock lid anymore. And hopefully, you will have eaten all your ferment before you notice any gasses building in the jar again.

> *NOTE ABOUT LIDS:*
> *This is not anywhere near an exhaustive list of lids. You may want to look up other types of lids such as Pickle Pipes, Masontops, Easy Fermenter, Bubble Airlock lids and more.*

Don't put a lid on it

Most of the foods in *Forty Days to Fermenting Success* use lids. But a few ferments require air to allow the microbes to work their magic. These include kombucha, water kefir and vinegar.

Although you'll need to let the air in, you'll also need to keep unwanted "shmutz" out... flies, dirt, mold, etc.

A simple piece of tightly woven breathable cloth, such as 100% cotton calico, fastened with a rubber band, works well. Don't use something with big air holes like cheesecloth. That won't protect your food from fly eggs, which could pass right through the holes in cheesecloth. You may also use a paper coffee filter or paper towel secured with a rubber band.

Signs of life

Along the fermenting journey, you might start to see bubbles form for a while then stop. Sometimes the bubbles are so tiny, you don't notice them as they wind their way up through the tangle of fermenting foods packed tightly in your jar. But they're there.

If you aren't using an airlock lid, and your jar is sealed tightly, you'll need to un-do the lid just a bit to let the gasses escape during the fermenting process. Listen for the strangely satisfying "pssst" as the gasses escape. Then screw your lid back down. Let the gasses out every time they build up or *(cue the scary music)* your ferment could explode like a volcano, spattering your ceiling, walls and favorite shirt with gloopy glop.

Sometimes your bubbles will do surprising things. For instance, as they form at the bottom or center of your container they might get stuck on their way up. When bubbles get wedged into the middle of your fermenting food, the pressure can push liquids upwards, squirting juice out the top – even with an airlock lid. That's why the most experienced PFC's put a plate or bowl under their jars.

Now don't worry if a bit of your juice escapes. Just gently give your jar a fist-bump or turn it over to release the bubbles. Or you can open the lid, pull out a bit of the ferment, eat it, and shove everything back down below the brine. Put back the follower and weight. Then reseal the lid.

Besides the bubbles, often you'll see the brine grow cloudy. That's another good sign of life. You'll watch the colors mingle and change. You'll smell the earthy tang of an evolving eco-system wafting through your fermentation chamber (or laundry room).

And as long as everything in your jar remains submerged below the liquid, it's unlikely that you'll see fuzzy black or green mold or a white wisp of yeast growing atop your food. If you do see a little bit, wipe it off completely, push your ferments below the brine and seal your jar back up.

NOTE ABOUT WATER AND SALT:
Fermentation involves living microbes. So you need to use ingredients that don't harm life.

Make sure your water is non-chlorinated, since chlorine kills bacteria.

As for your salt, use pure salt without added ingredients. And stay away from iodized brands. Iodine is something else that kills bacteria. Choose non-iodized salt for all your fermenting needs.

DAY FIVE: Salsa
(The food, not the dance… but don't let me stop you!)

Salsa is a quick 3 or 4 day ferment that you can personalize to your own taste. You can make a lot or a little. (I suggest making a lot because it's really really really good!)

Use salsa to:
Top your tacos, dress your salads, dip your chips and spoon on scrambled eggs and stir into guacamole. Don't stop there! Add flavor to poultry and pork. Spread a spoonful on meatloaf or hamburger. Make your zucchini stand up and beg. Spice up your soup and beans. Stuff your pasta shells. Impress total strangers with your fermenting skills.

Let's make enough for your next fiesta!

Tools:
- razor-sharp knife and cutting board (because tomatoes are finicky to cut)
- food processor/blender
- big bowl
- 3 quart-size glass jars with lids
- canning funnel (optional for aiming salsa into the jars)
- wooden tamper (optional, but really fun to play with)

Ingredients – include anything you think might suit your taste. My recipe came from an Irish-American friend who happened to have a special flair for making Mexican food! What do you like in your salsa? Well, then, put it in!

Here's a list of the fresh, organic foods that you might consider using in your salsa:

- 3 lbs. tomatoes, diced
- 1 or 2 sweet onions like (Walla Walla), half chopped for the bowl and half chunked for the blender
- yellow sweet peppers minced, discard seeds
- enough chopped hot peppers to your taste, discard seeds – I used two Poblano peppers and 2 little yellow hot peppers (don't rub your eyes or nose after handling!)
- minced garlic
- little squeeze of lime if you like a citrusy tang
- 1 tsp. cumin if desired – it's really delicious in your salsa
- 1 bunch of chopped cilantro, if desired
- 1 ½ tsp. non-iodized salt, or to taste

Place in a large bowl:
- diced tomatoes – let them sit in the bowl and drain for a little bit. You'll strain it later and transfer the juice to the blender with the onions, chilies and garlic.
- half of the chopped onions
- cumin
- cilantro
- salt
- any other ingredients you'd like in your salsa

Pulse together in your food processor until blended but still a bit chunky:
- juice that you strained from the tomatoes
- the other half of the onions, chunked
- chopped chili peppers to taste
- minced garlic
- lime juice, if using

Pour the saucy mixture from your food processor into bowl with the chopped tomatoes, onions, herbs, spices and salt. Stir well.

> *NOTE ABOUT SPECIAL TOOLS:*
> *Filling your jars with a canning funnel will help keep the messies down to a minimum. Big mouth funnels can be found at some hardware stores and "marts" in the canning section.*
>
> *The other specialized tool you may enjoy getting is a wooden tamper. Not only does it make you look really cool as you pound the air out of your fermenting jars, but you can also keep it by your bedside for protection at night… in place of that baseball bat you have there now.*

Fill your clean, quart sized jars, tamping down the salsa as you go to remove air. I like to use a wooden tamper tool for this, as it reaches deeply into the jars and pushes everything down evenly under the juice. Leave just about an inch of headspace at the top of the jar.

Use smaller jars if you need to, so that you don't have a big space at the top. Less air in your jar means less chance of growing mold!

Attach lids. Place jars in a pan/bowl/plate to catch drippings. Wipe clean and stow in your fermentation chamber (aka old bookcase in the laundry room) away from cold or heat. Depending on the temperature of your house, leave the jars for 3 to 5 days. Longer if it's on the chilly side, or if you like your salsa extra tangy.

When you check on your salsa tomorrow, you might see the juice in the bottom separated from the chunks at the top. No worries. Just tip the jars and shake gently to mix it all back together. Do this as often as twice a day. Shake things up and you'll prevent any mold from trying to steal your salsa. Ha!

If you're using an airlock lid, you won't need to burp your jars each day. Just be sure to shake or swirl gently as often as twice a day.

If you're using other lids, **don't forget to burp your jars daily** to release the gasses that are building up as a result of healthy fermentation.

When fermenting is complete, put a regular lid on your jars and refrigerate.

> *NOTE ABOUT LEFTOVERS:*
> *If you are lucky, you'll have more salsa left over than you can get into three jars. So... give yourself a treat! Scoop the rest into a salsa bowl and use it fresh on chips, or anything else that is begging for some spicy deliciousness.*

The great thing about fermenting your salsa is not only the improved digestibility, tangy taste and probiotic goodness, but also that it keeps for months in your refrigerator.

Day Five of your *Forty Days to Fermenting Success* turned out pretty awesome!

In just a few days, you'll have a supply of salsa you can be very proud of, not just for the taste, but also for the health benefits of the probiotics you've created in each jar.

Your fermented salsa is preserved without adding chemicals. That means it will taste delicious for weeks – unless you eat it all up before then.

Of course, once you have salsa, you gotta get the bean dip...

Turn the page to Day Six to make a super-simple, smooth and tangy dip we call "Musical Fruit."

DAY SIX: The "Musical Fruit"
(non-refried bean dip)

Do you have a favorite bean dip? Then you already have a head start! Just whip up a batch as usual, then add a starter like whey or a dollop of live-culture miso paste. Miso paste is found refrigerated in the Asian food section of your grocery store.

Blend the starter into the bean dip, then pour it into a clean jar. Add a lid and tuck away for a couple of days. You'll see it puff up as it ferments, fills with new flavors, and re-texturizes perfectly for balancing on a chip, cracker or toasted pita bread.

If you don't have a favorite bean dip, or you would like to try something different, here is my version of a fermented fiesta-worthy bean dip to serve at picnics, parties and for snacks.

Ingredients:

(Adjust to taste)
- 2 cans of organic pinto beans, black beans, or mixed rinsed and and drained (or cook your own)
- 1 fresh, seeded, diced jalapeno pepper, or pepper sauce to taste
- 1 teaspoon mild red chili powder
- pinch of cumin
- 3 to 5 fresh chopped green onions
- garlic powder to taste
- 1 teaspoon of live-culture miso paste, or 1 tablespoon of whey or other starter
- 1 teaspoon non-iodized salt (or to taste)
- pepper to taste

Process:

1. Place all ingredients in your blender and process till smooth.
2. Pour the bean dip into clean jars. Add a lid and tuck away for 2 days.
3. Burp your lids each day. Continue to ferment until you like the flavor.
4. When it's finished, put your bean dip into the refrigerator to stop the fermenting and start the party.

Next on the menu!

Coming up, we're going to make a batch of something smooth, thick and creamy that you can enjoy using for a dip, salad dressing or topping. And it goes beautifully with salsa and bean dip, on burritos and tacos, and atop a pile of fruit.

You'll be an overnight success with this next recipe.

DAY SEVEN: Kefir Cheese over the top!

I love to pair the fire-extinguishing taste of sour cream with spicy salsa.

But I've found something else that's just as creamy, tangy and tasty – and it's fresh made at home. Plus it's filled with health-promoting probiotics. That would be kefir cheese.

When I hear "cheese" I think two things:
   1. "Who's taking my picture?"
   2. "That's hard to make."

But no one is taking my picture, and kefir cheese is so easy.

When you make it from store-bought milk kefir, most of the work is done for you. All you need to do is let it drip through a paper coffee filter overnight. The end.

First I'm going to show you how to make kefir cheese from store-bought milk kefir. Then, on Day Eight, I'll tell you how to make your own milk kefir. Deal?

Instructions:

1. Line a sieve with paper coffee filters. Here I have a special Donvier brand setup with a sieve built into a receptacle especially for making Greek yogurt or kefir cheese. But all you really need to do is hang a sieve over a bowl and line it with paper coffee filters.

2. Next, pour your milk kefir into the filter-lined sieve. Cover and leave at room temperature or in the refrigerator overnight.

3. When it's all done dripping, you'll have something like sour cream in your coffee filters, plus a lovely puddle of almost clear, golden tinted whey in the bottom of the bowl.
See side note for ways to use your leftover whey >>>

NOTE: SAVE THE WHEY!

(I should have a bumper sticker made with that on it.) The whey that comes from straining milk kefir and yogurt is very nutritious and useful. I've included a few suggestions for how to use your extra whey on Day Thirteen, "Hey, Hey, Too Much Whey."

DAY EIGHT -- Make your own milk kefir

If you just finished making kefir cheese from store-bought milk kefir, then the cost of that little bottle of yumminess is fresh in your memory. It was probably sitting close to a similar sized carton of milk that cost a quarter of the price.

Compared to homemade milk kefir, store-bought kefir will contain a lower diversity of bacteria, and be less flavorful.

To sum up

Store-bought: more expensive, less nourishing, bland taste.

Homemade: one quarter the price, probiotic powerhouse, and rich, tangy flavor. Plus you can make it with a variety of milks… cow, goat, sheep, etc. Raise your hand if you're ready to make your own. I see that hand!

Gotta get the grains

Once you get your hands on some milk kefir grains, the process is so easy a caveman can do it… and probably did!

NOTE: Talking about "grains," kefir grains are not actual grows-on-the-end-of-a-stalk grains. They're just called grains because that describes how they look, in a nice way. It's so much nicer than calling them "rubbery, lumpy blobs," which is really how they look -- with some stringy slime thrown in. But that wouldn't be nice to say, would it? So they are called "grains."

To locate some milk kefir grains, put a call out to your community help page. See if you can find some "live" ones locally. If not, order some online. I got mine from Yemoos Nourishing Cultures and, I kid you not, they came with an Adoption Certificate.

Some people have luck with ordering the dehydrated grains. Many companies sell them. But for some reason, I could not get those things to perk up. I must have done something wrong.

After you get your grains, making kefir is one of those Ever-So-Easy ferments. No cooking. No heating. Just plop your goopy little grainy friends into a jar of raw or pasteurized milk (don't use ultra-pasteurized), cover with a loose lid, cloth or coffee filter, and set it out at room temperature to culture.

Once they've adapted to your environment, those little guys will culture your milk into kefir in 24 hours or less.

You may start out with a tablespoon or quarter cup, which cultures a cup or two of milk at a time. They'll continue to multiply.

As they increase in volume, you increase the amount of milk you use to feed them each 12 to 24 hours. You'll know they need more milk because your milk will culture faster than 12 or 24 hours. Add another half cup of milk and see how they do. Keep adding a half cup of milk each time they grow.

When the grains congregate at the top of your jar, and the milk looks slightly separated from the whey, your kefir is probably ready to shake and strain. Taste to be sure it's tangy.

Tighten your lid, shake the jar, and then pour your thickened milk kefir through a non-metal strainer and into a bowl. It's thickened, so you need to be patient. Wait for it. Give your strainer a little wiggle. Wait for it. Shove it around with a wooden spoon to help it drain.

Pour your freshly strained kefir into a container and put it in the refrigerator. Pour some fresh raw or pasteurized (not ultra pasteurized) milk into a clean jar and plop your goopy little grainy friends back into that jar of fresh milk. Put on the lid and set it out at room temperature to culture again for 24 hours or less.

Do a second ferment for carbonation and milder flavor

Your kefir is ready to drink after straining out the grains from the first ferment. It will be thick, creamy and tart, much like yogurt.

But you can do a second ferment that carbonates your kefir and mellows out the tanginess a bit. Just pour your finished kefir into a jar, put on a tight lid, and let it sit at room temperature another 6 to 12 hours. You can add a piece of fruit to flavor your kefir. Adding fruit will also feed the bacteria and increase the vitamins and probiotics. It will develop a bit of carbonation in the process.

You might see the whey separate after a second fermentation. Let out the gas by twisting the lid open. Then close it tightly and shake. Blend in fruit, jam, maple syrup or anything else you'd like to flavor it with. Refrigerate.

As your milk kefir grains grow and multiply, you'll soon have enough to divide the original colony and do some experiments using different kinds of milk if you like. And you'll have enough to give to your friends.

What can you do with milk kefir?

- Drink your kefir plain, or blend it with fruit.
- Turn that fruity kefir into popsicles or ice cream.
- Drizzle in some maple syrup or other sweetener.
- Soak your overnight oats in it, in place of water and yogurt.
- Make kefir cheese (a lot like sour cream).
- Use it as a base for salad dressings, especially good in anything that calls for buttermilk or yogurt, like ranch dressing.
- Stir it into muffin batter and zucchini cakes.
- Did you know you can even make bread, pizza dough and flour tortillas with milk kefir? (See DAY THIRTY-SIX on "FAKE SOURDOUGH")

DAY NINE – A fizzy fruity whey to go!

Let's use up some of that kefir whey you've been collecting. The sooner you use it, the fresher this special drink will taste. This recipe is one of our grandchildren's favorite treats!

Fizzy Citrus Drink – makes a quart

You've already got the kefir whey, so all you need to add to your mix is some fresh squeezed citrus juice (your own or from the store), a bit of organic sugar, and some non-chlorinated water to make a healthy beverage everyone can enjoy.

The sugar you stir into your juice, whey and water can be white or brown – organic and pure. Most of the sugar is "eaten up" during the fermentation process, leaving you with a softly sweet, mildly tangy carbonated beverage.

Here's a recipe for a quart of Fizzy Lemonade. It also works for grapefruit, orange or lime juice. Or even a mix of fruits! After it goes into the refrigerator, you'll need to drink it within a week for optimum flavor.

1. In a quart-sized container, completely dissolve ¼ **cup of sugar** and **¼ tsp non-iodized salt** in **½ cup of hot water**.
2. Add around 2 cups **cool water**. Make sure the mixed liquid is below 85 degrees. Your good microbes will die if there's too much heat.
3. Pour in **2 cups of organic citrus juice**.
4. Add **2 tablespoons of fresh liquid whey**, drained from milk kefir or live, active cultured yogurt. The whey should be fresh and contain live cultures.
5. Using a funnel, pour the mixture into a flip-top bottle or juice jar with a tight lid. Fill to the shoulder of the bottle, leaving about two inches of headspace at the top and close up the lid. (You can add a little water to bring it up to the shoulder.) Too little headspace and your bottles will explode! Too much headspace and they don't carbonate well.
6. Mark the date on your bottle and let it sit at room temperature for about 2 to 4 days burping it daily to release gasses. Each day it will turn tangier and less sweet.
7. Refrigerate and drink within a week's time.

> *NOTE: You can expand your variety of flavored fizzy drinks by using other kinds of fruit, or some natural, organic jam in place of the citrus juice. I've even made this with reconstituted frozen concentrate. Be patient if it doesn't carbonate right away. Some whey is more active than other whey.*

Sound the trumpet!

Now, get ready for **Day Ten** – you're about to create the quintessential ferment that

- fed the builders of the Great Wall of China;
- helped prevent scurvy in the long sea voyages of 18th century explorers; and
- reduced death from smallpox during the Civil War.

It's easy to make.
It defends you against toxins.
It breaks down starches, proteins and
fats in your gut.
It's not a bird.
It's not a plane.
It's … SAUERKRAUT!

DAY TEN: Sauerkraut is bully

"My father, who taught me (to ferment) said
'Sauerkraut is the broom that sweeps the stomach.'"
— Stan Krupp, lifelong fermenter

Sauerkraut could be called the "gateway ferment," you might say. That's probably because it's so simple, and it doesn't take any special ingredients. Cabbage and salt is about as basic as you get. I've even made a batch without the salt!

Once you get the process for fermenting sauerkraut under your belt, you've learned the basics of most other vegetable and fruit ferments.

Unlike the overnight soaked oats we made on Day Two, and the quick fermenting salsa we made on Day Five, sauerkraut takes several weeks to a month or more to go through the fermentation process.

The length of time you ferment sauerkraut depends on how sour you like it to end up, what the temperature is in your fermenting chamber (alright, alright, it's a laundry room!), whether you added a "starter," and whether you opted to feed your microbes with some higher carbohydrate veggies or fruits such as pineapple, carrots, apples or raisins.

Is it worth the waiting? Health, yes!

If you want to tip the outcome of the battle for health in your favor, then populating your gut with probiotics is a great place to start. Not just with supplements, though. When you eat your probiotics in live, fermented foods, you're not only getting a tremendous variety of lively probiotics, but also the prebiotics – the fiber that they feed on — all in the same mouthful.

Chawing down on sauerkraut not only gives you a rosy glow, but it also builds up good-guy strength in your microbiome (mouth, skin, gut and other addresses throughout your body). Then the good guys have the strength they need to fight the good fight … for your life.

Who sez?

The National Institutes of Health launched "The Human Microbiome Project" (HMP) in 2007. (See: https://commonfund.nih.gov/hmp) The Common Fund's HMP developed research resources to enable the study of the microbial communities that live in and on our bodies and the roles they play in human health and disease.

The following quote comes from an article from the Baylor College of Medicine, one of the centers working on the HMP with the National Institutes of Health:

"Although bacteria are often associated with infections, the bacteria that colonize the surface and insides of our bodies are essential for life. We are dependent on these bacteria to help digest our food, produce certain vitamins, regulate our immune system, and keep us healthy by protecting us against disease-causing bacteria."
https://www.bcm.edu/departments/molecular-virology-and-microbiology/research/the-human-microbiome-project

Baylor College of Medicine confirms that bacteria are necessary for health. And Harvard Health tells us where we can get them. The following quote from Dr. David Ludwig comes from an article called "Fermented Foods Can Add Depth to your Diet:"

"Live cultures are found not only in yogurt and a yogurt-like drink called kefir, but also in Korean pickled vegetables (called kimchi), sauerkraut, and some pickles. The jars of pickles you can buy off the shelf at the supermarket are sometimes pickled using vinegar and not the natural fermentation process using live organisms, which means they don't contain probiotics. To ensure the fermented foods you choose do contain probiotics, look for the words 'naturally fermented' on the label, and when you open the jar look for telltale bubbles in the liquid, which signal that live organisms are inside the jar."

https://www.health.harvard.edu/staying-healthy/fermented-foods-can-add-depth-to-your-diet

That's a big deal. When you've got a well-populated microbiome, balanced in your favor, your gut buddies can multiply, thrive, adapt and help your body block sickening bacteria that are trying to invade your innards and weaken your vitality.

Sauerkraut for the win

In the next few pages, you'll find instructions for making about two quart-sized jars-full of sauerkraut. (Depending on how big your head is. Cabbage head. You knew that.)

From the moment you begin to massage your cabbage shreds, you'll be adding diversity to the gut buddies you're about to grow. The microbes from your hard working hands will be added to the food you're creating. A bit of "you" will be in each bite.

The rest of the bacteria occur naturally on organic produce. That's one good reason to buy organic if you can. If your food is irradiated or soaked in bacteria killing products, your vegetables will be devoid of what they need to ferment.

Basic Cabbage Sauerkraut

Ingredients
Around 1200 grams (2.5 lbs) fresh organic cabbage
Non-Iodized Salt, about 2% of the weight of the cabbage, or to taste
Seasoning as desired

Tools
Big bowl, sharp knife, cutting board, scale, pounder, weight, jar and lid

The Process

1. Gather your tools and ingredients.

For seasonings, I like the flavor of caraway seeds, juniper berries and mustard seeds. Use whatever your taste buds ask for.

2. Reserve two outer leaves for later.

Cut your cabbage into 4 pieces and remove the hard center stem.

3. Slice your cabbage into thin, even pieces. That way all your sauerkraut will ferment at the same pace. Thinner slices help bring out more juices. But perfection isn't necessary.

Scoop all your cabbage into a big, BIG bowl.

4. At this point, you may simply salt to taste. Most people like the way a 2% brine works in sauerkraut. To make a 2% brine, you can weigh your sliced cabbage, and calculate 2% of the weight to determine the amount of salt it takes.

My cabbage came out to 1279 grams.
To figure 2%, I multiplied
$1279 \times 0.02 = 25.58$ grams of salt needed

5. I measured out 26 grams of finely ground pink Himalayan salt, which came to just a bit over a tablespoon. Since most salts vary in texture, and since tablespoon measurers are unreliable, it's best to weigh the salt rather than spoon-measure it.

Just about any pure, mineral-rich salt will do, as long as it doesn't have any added chemicals like iodine or anti-caking agents.

6. Sprinkle in salt and seasonings. Using your clean hands, mix the salt and seasonings into the cabbage. Human hands can add a little DNA to the mix that creates a special flavor unique to the ferments you create.

Let it sit and sweat for about 30 minutes or more while the salt draws the juice out of the cabbage. The salty juice will become your brine.

7. After waiting 30 minutes or so, dig in with both hands and firmly massage the cabbage. The massage will draw out more juice, and break down the cabbage to bring out the naturally sweet flavor. When the cabbage has wilted and you have a substantial puddle in the bottom of your bowl, you can start packing the cabbage into a clean jar.

8. As you fill your jar, tamp the cabbage in tightly. This will encourage even more juicing, and discourage air from getting into your ferment, which should ferment *anaerobically* (without air). Pour the juice left over in the bottom of your bowl into the filled jar. Leave just a couple of inches of headroom in the top. The space allows room for gasses and expansion of the sauerkraut.

If your cabbage didn't make enough juice, you can pour a little bit of 2% brine into the jar to top it off. Make a 2% brine by adding about a teaspoon of salt to a cup of water.

10. Top the sliced cabbage with the cabbage leaf you reserved earlier. The leaf is meant to help hold all the chopped cabbage down under the brine. Push the leaf down until the brine covers it.

It's good if your leaf has stiffness to it so that the pressure on the sides of the jar holds it in place.

"Under the brine, your ferment is fine."

11. Add a weight on top of the leaf. It can be a glass disk weight, or even a clean rock. Just something to help hold the chopped cabbage and leaf under the brine so that it can ferment anaerobically.

Any part of the vegetable poking out above the brine could possibly be a victim of mold, just as if it were sitting out in your compost pile. The salt in your brine can help protect your vegetables from rotting.

12. Screw on your lids – but not so tightly that they will be impossible to get off. Just a slightly firm twist will do.

Date your jars, set them on a pan or in a bowl to catch drips, and tuck them away in a spot with a consistent temperature – between approximately 68 and 72 degrees. That's just a "ballpark" estimate of ideal temperature. Just remember that the warmer it is, the faster the ferment, and that's not always a good thing.

13. Burp your jars daily as needed to release gas.

> *NOTE ABOUT LIDS:*
> *If you are using airlock lids (as described on Day Four), you won't need to "burp" your fermenting fruits and vegetables. If you use airtight lids, be sure to burp them daily to let out the naturally occurring gasses.*

Is my sauerkraut done?

Taste your sauerkraut after a few days to see if you like the flavor. If you want it to ferment a little longer and you have airlock lids, press your sauerkraut below the brine and pump out the air.

If you don't have airlock lids, just make sure your fermenting food is below the brine. Keep fermenting till you like the flavor! Some people let their kraut ferment for a week, a month or more. It's up to you. Your ferment, your choice.

The next time you try it, it will have matured a bit more. That means you'll be getting a different set of probiotics in this mouthful. A different set of flavors. A different texture. And that's a good thing!

When you like the taste, change out to a regular lid and move your jars to the refrigerator. Refrigeration slows the process of fermentation down, but doesn't stop it altogether.

When the time has come, how do you enjoy your kraut? Pile some of your probiotic-full sauerkraut on a baked potato, a cream cheese bagel, a buttered cracker or a plateful of scrambled eggs.

Make soup, add it to salad, stuff into a quesadilla. Wraps love sauerkraut. Pizza loves sauerkraut. There are dozens of way to enjoy it… and don't forget to pile it on your hot dogs, bratwurst and reuben sandwiches.

SAUERKRAUT IS BULLY

(An old folk song)

Now if you'll only listen to what I'm going to speak about,
I'm going for to tell you how to make the sauerkraut.
It isn't made of leather, as many one supposes,
But of the little flower which we calls the cabbage roses

Sauerkraut is bully. I tell you it is fine.
Methinks me ought to know it for me eats 'em all the time.

The cabbages are a-growin' so nice as nice can be.
Me takes 'em out and cuts 'em up in strips as you can see.
Me puts 'em in a kettle and me stamp 'em with me feet.
And me stamp it and me stamp it for to make 'em nice and sweet.

Sauerkraut is bully. I tell you it is fine.
Methinks me ought to know 'em for me eats 'em all the time.

Me puts in plenty of salt but me don't puts in no snuff.
Nor any cayenne pepper or any other stuff.
Me puts it in a barrel till it begins to smell.
So help me twice, we think it nice, the Dutchmen like it well.

Sauerkraut is bully. I tell you it is fine.
Methinks me ought to know 'em for me eats 'em all the time.

Now when sauerkraut starts to smell and it can't smell no smeller
Me take 'em from the barrel that's way down in the cellar
Me puts 'em in the kettle with speck till it begins to bile.
So help me you can smell 'er round for forty-thousand mile.

Sauerkraut is bully. I tell you it is fine.
Methinks me ought to know 'em for me eats 'em all the time.

DAY ELEVEN: Chutney, baby, are you getting sweet on me?

Day Eleven of your *Forty Days to Fermenting Success* will introduce you to a taste that's a wonderful surprise. A little sweet, a little savory, a lot of tangy flavors having a party in your mouth.

Let's chat chutney

Chutney is a side dish that originated in India. It's a very versatile condiment. You can spoon chutney onto a sandwich, alongside a plate of cold cuts and cheese, or into your meatloaf recipe. Dress up a plate of pork chops, stir it into a dip, pair it with curry dishes, pile it on a burger… and more. It's like a relish and it's like a jam and it's like a salsa. It serves to flavor up any meal or snack.

Usually made with seasonal fruit, vegetables and spices, a basic chutney goes together pretty easily. Chop. Season. Jar. But like any ferment you make, it's the waiting that's hard.

I found out with the first spoonful of chutney I made that the spices I put in there were amplified after fermenting. (I won't add that much cumin again…)

Chutney contradicts our ideas about what flavors go together. Until I tried it, I would never have paired peaches, apricots, nectarines, ginger and raisins with green onions and jalapeno pepper. But let me tell you… what flavor!

Depending on how tangy you want your chutney, you could be eating it anywhere from 3 to 10 days from now. Some people wait for several months. But if you taste it and you like it, hey, go get a spoon!

Step One

Head to the farmers' market, your garden or grocery store to pick up some in-season fruits, plus some veggies and spices you think might go with the flavors.

Step Two

In a big bowl, combine your chopped, diced ingredients. I've used apples and cherries, raisins and peaches and pears… You may find mangoes and pineapples, persimmons, apricots, cranberries and rhubarb.

I've de-seeded and diced jalapeno pepper, sweet pepper, sweet onion or leek and a bit of fresh, grated garlic, orange zest and ginger. You might use green tomatoes, red tomatoes, dried mustard and red pepper flakes along with a splash of apple cider vinegar.

Your chutney, your choice.

Then what about sprinkling in some cinnamon, cloves, star anise and a spoonful of sugar?

Or chopping up a few pecans for a crunchy surprise? Don't forget to squeeze in a lemon or two and grate in a bit of the zest.

Sprinkle in salt to taste.

Step Three

Stuff all your ingredients into jars, tamping down to ease out some of the juices till they rise to the top. You might need to add some non-chlorinated water to cover all the fruits and vegetables. Some folks splash in some starter like whey or sauerkraut juice. It won't hurt, but you really don't need to add a starter. Leave an inch or two of room at the top. Screw on your lid.

Sometimes my diced fruits get excited, and want to float up above the water. Even when I add a glass weight – some of them sneak right past it! It's like having kids that want to run out in traffic. So one way to keep those little guys safe is to place a "follower" between the top of the diced ingredients and the weight. You can fold in a cabbage leaf as you did for sauerkraut (See step 10 on page 37). Or cut a piece of unbleached parchment paper to size. A piece of cheesecloth or other 100% cotton cloth could work. Try some rounds of apple or slices of lemon.

Then wait.

Put your chutney into hibernation at room temperature for a few days, depending on how warm your house is. Watch for the bubbles to begin that indicate signs of life. If you don't have an airlock lid, burp your jar each day. There's no harm in shaking it a little if the fruit and veggies separate from the brine, just as you did the salsa on Day Five.

After 2 days, taste your chutney. Do you like it? If yes, put it in your refrigerator. If it's not quite tangy enough, push the chopped ingredients back down below the brine and let it ferment until you like the taste.

A year of chutney!

This flavorful side dish – brought to life by your creative imagination – dresses up any meal.

It's especially welcome during the holidays, and can add a zest that turns a meal into a party.

I'm looking forward to making some of these tasty dishes:
- apple ginger chutney to go with pork on New Year's Day.
- pineapple chutney with ham in the spring
- mango barbecue chutney for the Fourth of July
- pumpkin chutney in the fall
- cranberry chutney with our Thanksgiving turkey
- And I can't wait to wrap up the year with a cheese plate and cold cut platter served with a spicy tomato chutney, sparkling with peppers and onions.

Party on, friends!

DAY TWELVE – Yogurt, I love you. I hate you.

I love yogurt because...

Yogurt's got protein, calcium, vitamins and probiotics. I can use it to make breakfast smoothies, fruit and granola sundaes, salad dressings and frozen desserts.

I can whip it up with dill, cucumber, lemon, garlic and salt and pepper to make tzatziki, which is perfect for dipping chips and spreading on pita bread sandwiches and pouring over veggies.

When I drip it through a filter I get thick Greek yogurt, much like a sweet sour cream. Stop me if you've heard all this before.

I hate yogurt because...

A quart of organic, live-culture yogurt costs me twice as much (or more) than a quart of regular milk. That's understandable because there's a lot of work involved in processing milk into yogurt.

Sadly, regular store-bought yogurt can contain questionable ingredients. They are SO sneaky with that pectin, guar gum and sugar especially in some brands marketed to kids. (e.g. Tiny plastic tubes with cartoon figures.) I won't even mention the chemicals they don't mention!

Many cups and quarts of yogurt on your market's shelves don't even have live cultures after they've been processed to death. So why bother to pay the high prices?

Making yogurt takes time, which I don't always have

Here's why making it at home can feel overwhelming:

1. First I have to heat the milk up to 180-195 degrees and babysit it at that temperature for 10 minutes to denature proteins (a process that allows proteins to form a more stable gel). But look out – milk can scald easily if it gets too hot.

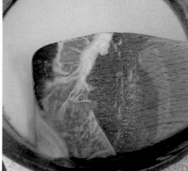

2. After that, I need to cool the milk back down (it takes approximately forever). When it gets down to 108 degrees, I wrestle it with a wooden spoon to skim off that gnarly skin. But the skin slips off each time I try to dig it out of the pot of milk.

3. From there, if I'm not crying yet, I pull some of the milk out of the pot and stir in a starter such as some yogurt from the store. Some store-bought yogurts will work to congeal the milk. But others have given me runny results. That's because some store-bought yogurt doesn't have live cultures. Or it's old and the cultures are worn out. I could pay top dollar to buy a package of powdered culture instead of using yogurt as a starter, but not many stores carry it.

4. If I've done everything right up to this point, it's all about the incubation – temperature and time. Here's where I need to pick a method to hold the yogurt mixture at around 108 degrees for however many hours it takes to firm up. Could be 4, 8, 10, 12 hours or overnight.

5. After working so hard to cook and cool and stir and incubate, I need to wait again while my yogurt cools down to room temperature before putting it into the refrigerator. If I don't wait, it could go all runny-funny on me, and we don't want that.

6. I'm tired just thinking about all those steps!

Shortcuts to the rescue!

In the search for an easier way to make home-made healthy yogurt, I wondered about whether I really needed to go through all those steps. Putting my finger on my chin, I asked, "If milk is pasteurized, why do I need to heat it before making yogurt?" Answer: Unfortunately, "pasteurized" only takes milk up to around 160 degrees – not enough to denature the proteins.

"On the other hand," I asked myself, "if it's *ultra-pasteurized,* the milk is heated to over 200 degrees. Would that do it?" Answer: You can't be sure that the milk you buy has been held at the higher temperature for 10 minutes, so the proteins may not form a stable gel. That would be something to test.

Tipping my head engagingly to the side, I then asked, "What about powdered milk? Has the protein in powdered milk been denatured? Would that help me skip another step in the process?" I'm feeling the need to test this process as well.

The testing begins

1. First experiment: I bought ultra-pasteurized organic whole-fat milk and didn't heat it. Into a quart jar of cold milk I added 2 tablespoons of good quality, active-culture yogurt. Then I screwed on a lid, and shook it well. After realizing that I hadn't put the lid on tightly enough, I mopped up the mess, then put the jar with its remaining contents into a warm spot to incubate. Would it turn into yogurt? Time would tell...

2. Second experiment: I bought nonfat powdered milk, mixed in water per the instructions to make about a quart, but used 30% more of the powder than it called for to be sure it was rich tasting. Then I added active-culture yogurt to the cold milk and SCREWED ON THE LID TIGHTLY. Finally I shook up the mixture until everything was smoothly combined, and put the jar into the same warm spot as the ultra pasteurized experiment.

3. Third experiment: In a saucepan, I heated pasteurized whole-fat milk to 190 degrees F, and held it there for 10 minutes. Then I let it cool to below 108 degrees F. For my last step, I stirred in the same active culture yogurt as #1 and #2, and put it in to incubate with the other two experiments.

NOTE: Five ways to keep yogurt warm while it cultures

1. Yogurt maker – You can buy loads of these at thrift stores. Many home cooks have donated their devices because they found out that they just couldn't keep doing these time-consuming steps week after week.

2. Instant Pot® – If you have one of these, you may already know how versatile this appliance is, including for yogurt making. You can have your pot do the whole thing for you: heating, cooling, and incubating. Or you can mix your inoculated milk into jars, set them on the trivet, push YOGURT button and keep them warm with a little water in the bottom of the pot. This is how I kept my experiments warm.

3. Sous Vide – This is a device that keeps a pot of water at an even temperature for as long as you set it for. It's usually used to slow-cook meats and grains in vacuum-sealed bags. But you can put your jars of milk, inoculated with live cultures from yogurt, into the sous vide set-up and let them sit in the warm water bath for as long as it takes for your yogurt to firm up.

4. Dehydrator – If you can fit your jars into a dehydrator that runs at around 110 degrees, then this will work.

5. A warm place in the house – like your oven with the interior light on. This gets a little involved because you need to put the inoculated milk into a jar, set the jar in a bowl of warm water, cover it all with a towel, and keep the water warm. When I did it, I left it in the oven (with the light on) overnight. It worked, eventually. You can also use a picnic cooler or ice chest and keep changing out the warm water in the bottom to keep jars warm.

For the test, I cultured the milk in jars and used an Instant Pot to keep all three of them warm at the same time so that the comparison would be fair.

Test results

1. The ultra pasteurized milk – which I didn't heat up before culturing – produced a nice, creamy, mild tasting yogurt. But it took 12 hours of culturing to get it to thicken. In the end, it tasted okay, but the consistency was a little bit runny. It thickened up a bit more overnight in the refrigerator.

2. The nonfat powdered milk, which I also didn't heat up before culturing, came out thicker than the ultra pasteurized experiment. I used BOB'S RED MILL® nonfat powdered milk. I detected a little bit of the distinctive powdered milk flavor in the yogurt. But it wasn't too bad. It took 10 hours of culturing to get it to set. I left it at room temperature for a bit before transferring the jar to the refrigerator. Overnight, it thickened up a little more.

3. Yogurt made in the traditional way (heating in a saucepan to denature the proteins before culturing) began to firm up quite a bit after only 5 hours of culturing. It tasted very creamy. I took the traditional yogurt out at 5 hours, let it come to room temperature, and put it in the refrigerator where it thickened up a bit more overnight. This was a clear winner for taste and texture.

What's your preference?

Using ultra-pasteurized and powdered milk lets you start your yogurt cold. It's quick to throw together, but takes a longer time to culture to get it to thicken up. Still, it's less time spent cooking and cooling and all that.

Traditional yogurt takes a lot more tending at the stove and less time in the warming chamber. But then again, there are very specialized yogurt makers these-a-days that can automate some of those steps for you.

My preference…

If I'm in a hurry, I'll make yogurt with powdered milk.
If I want the best taste, I'll take time to go the traditional route.

NOTE ABOUT LACTOSE FREE MILK:
You can make yogurt with ultra-pasteurized milk, powdered milk or regular milk. You can add cream for thickness and flavor.

But you can't go LACTOSE FREE – yogurt needs lactose to develop its tangy thick essence.

DAY THIRTEEN – Hey hey, too much whey!

If you've been making Greek yogurt or kefir cheese lately, then you just may have a bit too much whey building up in your refrigerator. Or freezer.

As a person who hates to waste anything, I researched how I could use my whey. Some ideas that I found included:

1. Soak your oatmeal in water and a little whey to make it more digestible.
2. Add a splash of tangy whey to your iced tea instead of lemon. (I didn't like it, but some people do.)
3. Blend it into smoothies to add flavor and increase nutrition.
4. Use it in recipes that call for milk or buttermilk.
5. Pour some whey into fruit juice, cap tightly and let it carbonate.
6. Use whey as a starter in fermenting fruits or chutneys.

But I wanted more ideas, because I had more whey than I knew what to do with. Surprisingly, I found out that the lactic acid in your whey is similar to the alpha-hydroxy acids found in expensive skin products.

That said, let's see what whey can do for your beauty regimen:

1. Use diluted whey on a cotton ball to remove dead skin cells wherever you may find them.
2. Add it to warm water in your sink to rinse your face.
3. Pour it into a bath and relax, knowing there are probiotic buddies swimming around with you. (This was nice!)
4. Treat your scalp to a healthy whey rinse.
5. Soak your cracked, peeling fingernails 10 minutes a day to help strengthen them. (Yes! It worked!)
6. Put some whey in a footbath to soften hardened skin. Follow up with a coating of coconut oil, and socks. Go to bed. In the morning, you'll either have soft feet or a cat licking your toes. Possibly both.

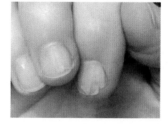

I used as much whey in these ways as I could. Still, I ended up with a full gallon of the stuff in my refrigerator. Let me show you what I did...

How to make salted caramel out of whey

This process isn't hard. It just takes a lot of time, waiting for the whey to evaporate and congeal. When I was done, I had five cups of tangy homemade caramel to share with family and friends. This stuff is just right for pouring over ice cream, dipping apples or smearing on pie.

*Please note that this recipe is for the acid whey you drain from your yogurt or kefir. It won't work with powdered whey or sweet whey.

Ingredients:

- 1 gallon of whey drained from yogurt or milk kefir
- 3 cups of sugar
- 1 teaspoon vanilla extract
- ¼ teaspoon of sea salt
- 8 ounces butter

Process:

1. Pour your gallon of whey into a large pot on the stove set at medium heat.
2. Let it simmer until the liquid is reduced by half.
3. Stir in sugar, vanilla, salt and butter. Keep an eye on it and stir often.
4. After about 45 minutes or more, the liquid will turn to a dark golden color. Keep stirring at this point so that your syrup won't burn. It will bubble and foam as it thickens up.
5. When it's thick enough to coat a spoon, remove it from the heat. As it cools, it will thicken up even more.
6. When it's cooled enough, pour into jars.
7. Store in the refrigerator, and warm before using.

If you can't use up your whey within a week or two after draining it out of your cultured dairy, you can freeze it.

DAY FOURTEEN – A new day, a new kind of sauerkraut

On Day Ten, you found out how easy it is to make sauerkraut... and that *Sauerkraut is Bully*. Like a parent with a newborn, you may have found yourself peeking in on the sleeping cabbage every now and then. If you used a regular lid, you'll have been burping it daily by letting out the gasses. Pssst.

I hope you were rewarded along the way by seeing the signs of life – bubbles, cloudy brine and possibly a bit of foam.

The sauerkraut may have swollen to the top of the jar and spewed its way out of the airlock, if you used one. Don't be shy about patting it back down under the brine if you need to. A little jostling doesn't hurt anything!

You may have even reached in with a tentative fork and tasted it. Was it getting sour? Did it taste salty or tangy? If you did open it, make sure to re-cover your veggies with brine and the weight. This will keep the fermenting process going.

Time to start your next batch

While your first batch is fermenting, it's time to start a second batch. But this time, let's experiment with flavors.

Follow all the basic instructions from making your first sauerkraut, with the following changes.

When you pile your chopped cabbage into a big bowl, toss in a chopped **apple,** and some cut up pieces of **pineapple.** (If you don't have fresh pineapple, frozen works too.) Grated **carrot** is a good addition as well. Sprinkle in your salt and let it sit and sweat for around 30 minutes as you did before.

Massage to release juices. Look for a juicy, briny puddle in the bottom of your bowl.

Before tamping it into jars, use a spoon or spatula to stir in some freshly grated **ginger** and **turmeric.** I'd estimate about two tablespoons of each, more or less, depending on your own tastes. If you don't have fresh, you can use powdered seasoning. The powdered seasonings are more concentrated than the fresh, so you won't use as much. Maybe just 2 teaspoons. Taste to see what you like.

Then tamp it all into jars as before. Pour in the extra brine from the bottom of your bowl. Add a cabbage leaf and a weight to hold veggies and fruits below the brine. Label your jars with the flavors you used and the date you put the lid on it. Set it in a dish to catch overflow.

I'm waiting…

The fruit you added may make your bacteria pretty excited. So they may jump into fermenting more quickly than your first sauerkraut. That just means you can reap the harvest a little sooner. (Not so much waiting!)

What if it's taking too long?

Adding certain spices to your ferments may make your bacteria a little shy! So they may hold back from fermenting right away. You just never know.

That's because the veggies and fruits are individual. They're harvested from different farms, families and seasons. The amount and type of wild bacteria that ride in on your produce will ebb and flow. Your home temperature will fluctuate. The juice and natural sugar in produce will not be constant.

So with all your ferments, keep a watchful eye (and nose). When it tastes good to you, move your sauerkraut to the refrigerator to slow down the fermentation to a Los Angeles Freeway crawl.

Each time you make a ferment recipe, it will be a little different. Watch. Sniff. Taste. Enjoy.

And don't forget to write down the recipes. If you hit on a genius flavor, you're going to want to make it again and again.

DAY FIFTEEN – Honey, got garlic?

Are you ready for another so-easy ferment? Honey-infused garlic, or garlic infused with honey – whichever you call it, that's what we're doing for Day Fifteen.

Two ingredients: Raw, organic honey and raw, organic garlic.

The hardest part of doing anything with fresh garlic might be separating the cloves and getting the skins off. I've looked at all kinds of suggestions on the Internet. Many of them include shaking the garlic inside bowls or jars. I say, go with what works for you.

Here's what worked for me:

1. After pulling/rubbing/peeling off the outer skin of the bulb, I took my handy tamper and pushed down on the garlic bulb to force the cloves apart.

2. I also used the tamper to slightly push down on the individual cloves, or I just bent them with my fingers, to crack or bruise them a bit. The skin came off pretty easily once the cloves were bruised or bent. Bruising the cloves causes them to release a bit of juice. The juice is going to mix with the honey and work some magic.

3. Pile your slightly bruised garlic cloves into a jar.

4. Pour honey over them to cover, then stir. Leave a few inches of headroom because this is a very lively ferment. It will try to escape through the nooks and crannies of the lid as it bubbles and expands.

5. Leave your honey-garlic infusion to ferment. Burp and turn the jar every now and then to release the gasses and keep the garlic coated with honey as much as you possibly can.

6. Your ferment will bubble and grow more liquefied as the garlic juice mingles with the honey. You can start to eat it in about a month. Don't try it too soon or you won't like the sting of garlic down your gullet. Wait for it to mellow and sweeten.

DAY SIXTEEN – Become a kvasnik in one easy lesson, or… why is my pee pink?

Non-chlorinated water. A little non-iodized salt. A couple of organic beets.

That's it. That's all that goes into making the simplest beet kvass. Cut 2 large beets into cubes. Drop them into a quart-sized jar of water with a half-teaspoon or more of salt. Stir to dissolve salt. Cover jar with a lid. (Remember to burp out the gasses each day while it ferments.)

Wait a few days or a week, swirling the liquid around now and then. Strain beets. Sip juice.

Once your first batch is done, you can even leave a little kvass in the jar for a starter and use the beets for a second batch. Just add water with a little salt, according to your taste. Cover. Wait. Swirl. Wait. Strain beets.

The second batch is not as strong as the first, but it still tastes very good.

What's it taste like?

My opinion is that beet kvass tastes a little, well, "earthy." But good-earthy. They call this an "acquired taste." That's why you'll see so many recipes online that add things to beet kvass before fermenting it. Apple, lemon, pear, ginger, spices… even horseradish. (I say "neigh" to the horseradish.)

After fermentation, kvass can be mixed with other beverages to make a delicious "kocktail," including sparkling water, water kefir and kombucha.

This deep, dark, maroon tonic is so strong in flavor and probiotic power that you'd be well advised to only sip a bit at a time, especially if you're not used to fermented foods yet. You can increase the amount you drink as you feel ready.

There are many different kinds of kvass, even some made with rye bread, but we'll just use beets as a "gateway kvass" today.

Why drink beet kvass?

Our friends at the National Institutes of Health (NIH) were concerned with a condition called "oxidative stress." That's what happens when people are exposed to too much heat, strenuous exercise, cancer and infectious pathogens. The NIH researchers looked for antioxidant food sources that have the ability to tackle the problem.

They found that beets are an exceptionally rich source of antioxidant compounds with really big unpronounceable names. To try and pronounce those names, you can look up the article about beets here: https://www.ncbi.nlm.nih.gov/pmc/articles/PMC4425174/

And in case you are interested, they found that beets are also good for lab rats.

In the same article by the NIH, they examined the problem of persistent, unresolved inflammation. One thing they mentioned was that using non-steroidal anti-inflammatory drugs can have some pretty bad side effects, and in the end are just not effective. That's why they started looking at natural food sources as an alternative to drugs.

Guess what they landed on? More big words about the "potent anti-inflammatory agents" in beets. Seems that something in beets alleviates inflammation and pain in osteoarthritic patients.

If this is interesting to you, keep your eye on the NIH. There are more studies to come, including one on how the compounds in beets may help with hypertension.

Why not drink kvass?

1. Compounds in beets are known to lower blood pressure. So those who already suffer from low blood pressure would be wise to drink responsibly – or avoid it altogether.

2. If you buy it in the grocery store, check the sugar content on the label. Store-bought kvass may not have gone through the traditional fermenting process. Buyers beware. When you make your own kvass, and you allow it to ferment for days or weeks, it isn't high in sugar.

3. According to Harvard Health blog, beets are in a category with chocolate, rhubarb, spinach, tea and most nuts that are involved in forming kidney stones in some people. If you suffer from stones, you'll want to limit how much of these foods you eat.

4. Lastly, pink pee. It's got a name: beeturia. After eating beets you may pass some pink stuff. This can signal low stomach acid that's not strong enough to break down the pigment in beets. And it can even warn you that you might have an iron deficiency.

Try making some beet kvass and see where you stand on the "earthy" taste. Use it as a tonic, drinking just a bit at a time. Ferment it with flavors, or mix it with other beverages.

For myself, I'm thinking of rinsing my silvery gray hair in a bit of beet kvass to impress my grandchildren. My adult kids don't think it's cool, but the four year old is on board with the idea.

When you get to be my age, you can give yourself permission to go a little wild.

Ingredients:

- organic beets, chopped (if beets are organic, no need to peel them)
- 1% brine solution (for each liter of non-chlorinated water, add 5 grams of salt – around a scant teaspoon)
- 1 tablespoon of starter from whey or a previously fermented food if desired

You may also add for flavor:
- apples, oranges, lemons, ginger, chili pepper, spices

Process (First fermentation):

1. Put chopped beets and flavoring ingredients into a jar, filling it ½ to ¾ full.
2. Fill the jar the rest of the way with 1% brine solution (one scant teaspoon of salt per quart of non-chlorinated water).
3. Cover with a lid.
4. Place the jar in a room-temperature area to ferment for 3 to 7 days, stirring or swirling occasionally.
5. When fermented to your liking, strain out the liquid.
6. Put the veggies and some of the fermented kvass back into the jar and fill again with a 1% brine solution, cover and ferment.
7. Drink small amounts, or dilute with club soda, kombucha, fruit juice…

Second fermentation:

1. You can drink the kvass as-is, or re-bottle it for a second fermentation in smaller swing top bottles.
2. Pour a small amount of fruit juice, some honey, or syrup into the bottles if desired.
3. Pour in your beet kvass, leaving 2 inches of headroom for the carbonation.
4. Close the lid tightly.
5. Wait one week, burping bottles occasionally as needed. Open carefully! Contents may be highly pressurized.

DAY SEVENTEEN – Hoochy koochy boochy

Kombucha, familiarly known as "Booch," is filling the market shelves – and the kombucha makers' pockets!

Have you discovered the fermented tea in the high priced bottle yet? It's very tangy. Gently carbonated. Slightly sweet. Sometimes flavored with fruits and roots.

If you like it, and you'd like to save a bundle, you can make it at home. But first you need to obtain a kombucha "SCOBY." That's the magical rubbery pancake that turns plain sweet tea into kombucha.

SCOBY stands for Symbiotic Colony Of Bacteria and Yeast. Places to get one include your friends, neighbors, the Internet and growing one yourself from a bottle of regular store-bought kombucha. All that goes into the formula is tea, sugar, a little kombucha from your previous batch, and a SCOBY.

Each time you brew a batch, the SCOBY grows a new layer. That's why your friends are happy to share. Their SCOBYs are multiplying, and if they don't give them away, they just have to toss them out into the compost pile or feed it to their dog.

What can I do with booch?

The main use for kombucha is to drink it. Straight or mixed with kvass or other juices. If you're paying $3 to $5 a bottle, you can't afford to do much more than drink it.

But if you're brewing your own, you'll pay less, and have a new batch every 7 days or so. If you have plenty, you can use it in the same way you might use vinegar in a salad dressing to add flavor. Or marinating meat. I've heard of people rinsing their hair with it.

And one day, when we had a ton of the stuff, my husband mixed it into a little warm water, soaked his feet, and gave himself a pedicure. Yes, he did.

One time I mixed it into a little bit of bread flour just to see if the yeast in the kombucha would cause it to rise – and it did! I made a little bun, and it tasted pretty good, too.

DIY (Do It Yerself) Booch

Following is a step-by-step explanation on how to make kombucha at home. It includes how to do a "second ferment." That's an extra step you may want to follow to induce more carbonation.

Kombucha Tea – First and Second Fermentation

Ingredients
Water
5 plain tea bags – no flavors or oils added
1 cup white sugar
SCOBY (**S**ymbiotic **C**ulture **O**f **B**acteria and **Y**east)
1.5 cups kombucha from a previous ferment or
purchased – such as GT's raw organic plain kombucha

Tools
Gallon jar scrubbed nice and clean
Kettle to boil water
Cloth or paper coffee filter and rubber band

1. Steep 5 black tea bags in about a quart of boiled water for 15 minutes or so.

2. Remove tea bags and dissolve one cup of sugar in the tea.

3. Add enough cold water to fill a gallon jar three-fourths of the way full. Ensure that the sweetened tea is below 85 degrees F. Higher temperatures may harm your SCOBY.

4. When cool, add 1 and a half cups of plain kombucha to the jar. Stir.

5. Gently place a live SCOBY on top of the tea. It may float or sink. It doesn't matter.

6. Cover the mouth of the jar with a clean tightly woven cloth (NOT cheese cloth, or fruit flies will get in) or a paper coffee filter and secure with a rubber band. It needs air to ferment.

7. Let the kombucha tea ferment in a clean room-temperature area away from direct sunlight for 7 to 14 days. Try not to disturb it. Make sure you have good air circulation for this ferment.

8. Taste your tea after a week. Try not to disturb the SCOBY when you do this. Some people slip a straw in below the SCOBY and draw out some of the kombucha. Or if your jar has a spigot, you can let some out into a cup and taste it.

If it's not tangy enough, taste again the next day. Let it continue to ferment until it's flavorful and a bit tangy. Don't let it go too long or it will taste sour and vinegary, and the good bacteria will be... R.I.P. (Dead.) You won't be able to accomplish a second ferment if the bacteria have died.

9. At this point, you may drink your kombucha as-is, or opt for a second ferment in sealed bottles to develop more flavor and carbonation. Whichever you decide, be sure to reserve 1.5 cups of brewed kombucha for starting your next batch of sweet tea.

10. Second fermentation is easy – just pour your brewed kombucha into single-serving size bottles, add any flavorings you desire, and cap tightly. Check every few days and relieve pressure. When it develops the carbonation you desire, move the bottles to the refrigerator.

NOTE ON SECOND FERMENTATION:
- *Carbonation creates pressure inside the bottle, so be sure to use bottles that are especially made to withstand pressure, like the swing-top bottles made for brewing beer.*
- *You can flavor your booch during your second fermentation by pouring in pure, organic juice about one-fourth of the total volume, then fill the rest of the way with your booch. Leave a couple of inches of headspace. Give the gasses some room to accumulate.*
- *Burp your jars as needed to prevent too much carbonation from forming. In hot weather, that could be daily!*

DAY EIGHTEEN – Water kefir:
The burpin' Grammy's choice

While you wait for 7 to 14 days for your kombucha to go through its first ferment, you might try mixing up a batch of water kefir, which ferments in 2 or 3 days.

Where kombucha's key essence is its tanginess, water kefir's charm comes from its fruity fizz. Water kefir appeals to kids as well as adults. At my house, I keep a supply of flavors such as "Apple Andy," "Blueberry Sal," "Peachy Keen," "Grape Scott," "Lemon Joe," and "O-K, O-J!"

The kids help themselves to the bottled beverages which they call "Burpin' Grammy Soda." Yep, I'm dang proud of spoiling the grands!

The first ferment ingredients are simple enough – water, sugar and some water kefir grains (not to be confused with milk kefir grains).

Water kefir will ferment for you in just 2 or 3 days. Then your second ferment, when you add the fruit juice and other flavors, will take another 2 or 3 days.

Where do water kefir grains come from?

These wacky-shaped rubbery diamond-sized globs are a colony of bacteria and yeast, similar to kombucha's SCOBY. Originating on plants, they're called by different names around the world such as:

- Japanese water crystals
- California (or Australian, or African or Ginger) bees
- Ginger beer plant
- Sea Rice
- Plitz
- Graines Vivantes
- Tibicos
- Eternity Grains
- Balm of Gilead

The different names may indicate slightly different species of the same sort of bacteria/yeast colony. The ones I use have been colonizing, growing and carbonating drinks for us since September of 2018. And they don't seem to be slowing down.

I bought mine from Florida Sun Kefir. They came in the mail along with an e-book containing very detailed care instructions and ideas for flavoring your fizzy concoctions.

As the water kefir grains multiplied (like Tribbles for you Star Trek fans), I was able to share with friends, neighbors and strangers in our community. Still, they grew so much that I started feeding them to my compost pile every now and then.

All that to say, you're not likely to experience a shortage of supply.

Eventually, when you go on vacation, you'll need to hibernate your little pals by packing them into some sugar water and letting them go to sleep in the refrigerator while you're gone. Even water kefir grains like to take a vacation.

Start small

In the following instructions you'll learn how to make water kefir in a gallon jar. If you want to make less, just do the math, divide in half or quarters and proceed from there.

Here are a few things that water kefir grains may be sensitive about:

- Don't use any metal to touch your water kefir. Get a non-metal sieve and spoon.

- Check the temperature of the water before you add live cultures. Keep it below 85 degrees.

- Water kefir grains love minerals and hate chlorine. Reverse osmosis filtered water will need you to add a tiny bit of minerals to it to feed your grains. Suggestions are made below.

- If your water kefir starts tasting a little "off," it may be leaning toward growing too much yeast. You can fix that by squeezing about a tablespoon of lemon juice in with the first ferment. Or drop in a slice of washed organic lemon.

- Another reason your water kefir may taste "off" is if you let the first ferment go too long. 48 hours is plenty.

Water Kefir – First Fermentation

Ingredients
- 1 cup of active water kefir grains per gallon of liquid (you can make smaller batches if you prefer)
- 1 cup of organic sugar, sucanat, turbinado or brown sugar per gallon of liquid
- Chemical free water – reverse osmosis water can be used if you add minerals. Kefir grains need minerals to feed on.

Tools
Jar, spoon, thermometer, measuring cup, cloth or coffee filter, rubber band

1. To make a gallon of water kefir, start by dissolving one cup of sugar in one cup of hot water. Stir well with a non-metal spoon.

NOTE ABOUT HONEY: Some people will tell you not to use honey when making kefir. They reason that raw honey has its own bacteria that can compete with water kefir grains. Some pasteurized honey is contaminated with high fructose corn syrup. If you want to try using honey, be sure to reserve some of your grains in case the experiment doesn't work out.

2. When your sugar is fully dissolved, add cool water three-fourths of the way up the jar and check the temperature of your liquid. If it's below 85 degrees Fahrenheit, you're good to continue.

3. Add a cup of kefir grains to the sugar water. If you would like to feed your grains a little more, (see note below on "To keep your kefir grains healthy") you can drop in a bit of dried, unsulfured fruit, or a slice of lemon. Every second batch, mineralize your water with a pinch of non-iodized salt or baking soda.

4. Cover your jar with a clean cloth or paper coffee filter to keep unwanted insects, dirt or other floaties from becoming part of your ferment. Then label your bottle with the date, and allow your kefir mixture to ferment in a moderate temperature for 24-72 hours.

TO KEEP YOUR KEFIR GRAINS HEALTHY:
As you make subsequent batches, <u>add in minerals every second batch</u> such as ONE of the following:
- *Pinch of baking soda*
- *Pinch of natural, non-iodized salt*
- *1/8 teaspoon of molasses*
- *dried, unsulfured fruit such as figs, apricots or raisins*
- *Lemon slice or teaspoon of lemon juice*

Water Kefir – Second Fermentation

In this step, the living kefir microbes consume the sugar in the fruit or juice. This could take anywhere between 24 and 72 hours depending on the liveliness of your kefir, and the temperature of the air. The result is a fizzy, not too sweet, probiotic drink. My grandchildren go nuts for blueberry water kefir!

Ingredients
- The water kefir that you made
- Juice or fruit or other flavors to add
- A bowl of clean water

Tools
Sieve, large pitcher, large bowl of clean water, funnel, swing top bottles or juice jars with tight lids

1. Gather together your non-metallic tools and the jar of water kefir that you made 24 to 72 hours ago.

2. Pour fermented water kefir with grains through a sieve, reserving the liquid in a pitcher.

3. Transfer kefir grains into a bowl of clean, cool water. Let them rest for 20 minutes while you make the flavored water kefir. You will be straining them out again to start a new batch after you make your bottled drinks.

4. You may drink your water kefir as it is, or do a second fermentation to add carbonation and fruit flavors.
For the second fermentation, pour organic juice, fruit or other flavorings into a clean, swing top bottle or other jar with a tightly fitting lid.

Experiment with flavors to find out what you enjoy best.

5. Pour water kefir in with your juice, fruit or other flavorings. Stop filling at the shoulder of the bottle. Secure the cap. Reserve some of the water kefir to add back into your next batch.

6. Label your bottles with the date and flavor. Set your bottles in a moderate temperature (68 to 72 degrees F) area to commence a second ferment. Some people put their bottles in a sealed picnic chest – just in case of an explosion. That way the mess is contained.

7. To start a new batch, drain your grains out of the bowl of water and go back to the instructions for Your FIRST Fermentation.

Your grains will multiply. The next time you strain out the kefir grains, you may see tiny baby grains starting. Don't throw them out. They will keep growing and multiplying. Pass your extra kefir grains on to a friend. Blend them into a smoothie. Or compost them in your garden.

DAY NINETEEN – Kimchi: Kissin' kousins with kraut

Day Nineteen in your *Forty Days to Fermenting Success* will introduce you to a traditional fermented food from the Asian continent: kimchi. Like sauerkraut, there are hundreds of ways to make kimchi. Both sauerkraut and kimchi are made with cabbage, but the two differ in a few ways.

The main ingredient in sauerkraut is shredded cabbage – usually the kinds that grow in tight heads. It's *usually* fermented for anywhere from a week, up to 6 weeks and longer at medium room temperature.

Kimchi uses Chinese cabbage – like Napa or bok choy – combined with various herbs and spices. Many people eat it "fresh" (not fermented) in a bowl of fried rice.

> *TEXT FROM A FRIEND:*
> *Dear Sue, "Fresh" is not kimchi.*
> *Sincerely, Daniel*

When fermented, kimchi is often left at relatively cool room temperatures *usually* for about 3 weeks. The length of time for any ferment can vary according to a number of factors including:

- the temperature in your fermentation space (under the bed, atop the fridge, tucked into a book case, closed into a picnic cooler, etc.)
- the liveliness of the bacteria present (on your veggies, your hands, your kitchen)
- the types of herbs and spices you are using (some spices slow or speed up fermentation)
- the prebiotics included in the recipe (carbohydrate-rich fruits and veggies ferment faster)
- how thinly you slice your veggies (thinner slices release more juice)
- the amount of salt you use (more salt means slower fermenting, and that's not especially a bad thing)
- how sour you like your fermented food to end up

Sauerkraut is tart and refreshing. Kimchi is sour and spicy.

Sauerkraut may take less than one hour to chop and salt the cabbage and pack into a jar. Traditional kimchi has a few more steps, as you'll see in the recipe that follows.

BOTH are full of fiber, vitamins and probiotics that benefit your health.

Of course, everyone has their own versions of both sauerkraut and kimchi – and as long as you like what you make, it's all good.

Some of my friends love to include fish sauce and fermented shrimp in their kimchi recipe creations. Other friends tell me they prefer an all-vegetable concoction. Some people leave the leaves of the cabbage intact and roll them up into the jar. Others chop the cabbage into bite sized bits.

But that's just a few ways that I and my buddies do it. You can do whatever you like, and that's the best way to go. We can still be buddies, no matter how you make your kimchi.

Discover your preference through experimenting with various tastes. You never know what's going to tickle your taste buds and pickle your innards 'til you grab a fork and go for it.

The following directions are very basic and come hard-won by the process of my multiple failures. Make your own mistakes, and correct as you go. Don't give up. There's a delicious surprise right around the corner.

> *TEXT FROM A FRIEND:*
> *Dear Sue, The kimchi you made for me could use a bit more spice in it. Quite a bit more spice in it.*
> *Sincerely, Daniel*

BASIC KIMCHI

Here's a recipe for basic kimchi without fish sauce or shrimp. When I got finished, I had 5 quart-jars full of mild, but pretty tasty kimchi.

Veggie ingredients:
- 2 large heads of Napa cabbage
- salt to taste
- several green onions, chopped
- a big handful of matchstick-chopped daikon radish
- a big handful of matchstick-chopped carrots
- 1 Fuji apple, chopped

For the porridge:
- 3 cups of water
- three-fourths cup of white rice flour
- 2 tablespoons of sugar, brown or white (optional)
- hot pepper flakes (gochugaru)
- hot pepper paste (gochujang)
- a 2-inch knob of peeled, chopped ginger
- several cloves of peeled garlic (per your own taste)
- one medium-sized onion quartered

Tools:
- knife
- cutting board
- gigantic bowl
- pounder
- jars and lids
- stove
- saucepan
- blender
- something like a lasagna pan to set the jars in for fermenting (catches juicy eruptions)

The Process

1. Gather your ingredients.

2. Make a slit into the stem of your cabbages and gently pull them apart.

3. Make a second slit in the stem of each half so that you can easily bend the leaves out for salting, but keep the upper part of the stem intact so it still holds the leaves together.

4. Wet cabbage halves. Shake the excess water off and then sprinkle salt on each layer of leaves while gently separating, but leaving them attached to the stem. The salt you use now will start to pull the juice out of the cabbage leaves by osmosis. The wilting process will begin. Later, you'll be rinsing salt off of leaves, so don't worry a lot about getting too much salt on there now.

5. Set the cabbage halves into a big bowl and visit them every 20 minutes or so to turn over and slightly massage as you turn. They will release their juices over the next two hours. Reserve the brine that puddles in the bottom of the bowl in case you need it later to fill the jars to the top with liquid.

6. In the meantime make a "porridge." Start by adding the water and rice flour to a saucepan. Stir well and bring it to a boil, cooking until the liquid thickens up like a gravy.

7. Stir in optional sugar.

8. Let the porridge cool before adding it to your blender with the garlic, ginger, and onion. Blend until smooth.

9. Add some chili paste and chili powder to the porridge if you want your kimchi to be spicy. For an authentic flavor, use Korean pepper flakes – gochugaru and Korean pepper paste -- gochujang. At this point, if you like fish sauce or shrimp, blend these in as well.

10. Back to the cabbage… It's been wilting by releasing its juice for about 2 hours. It's time to drain out the salty brine and reserve it in a bowl for later. Next, rinse your wilted cabbages in clear water. You can fill your sink or a small tub up with water and soak the cabbages if you like. Drain the water and rinse again. Rinse a third time. Then drain well.

11. Slice the tough stem off the cabbages. You may want to chop and save these lovely, crunchy stems and use in a salad (delicious).

12. At this point, tear your cabbage into pieces. Toss the chopped green onion, daikon radish, carrots and chopped Fuji apple into the torn cabbage and stir in the porridge. When everything is mixed well, place all your vegetables into a jar or crock. Use gloves to protect your hands if you are sensitive to the peppers.

13. Pack your vegetables tightly into jars using your tamper. The point is to get the air out and all the veggies packed in tightly. Leave about 2 inches of space at the top.

14. The juice should rise to the top as you pack the kimchi into your jars. Add a weight to keep everything submerged. The juice should come above the weight. If you don't have enough juice to cover, pour in some of your reserved brine. Just make sure everything is submerged.

15. Cover jars with a lid, and place them into a pan or bowl to catch the overflow of juice as your kimchi ferments. If you have airlock lids, the juice will bubble out the top and no

air will flow in. If you have regular canning lids, be sure to "burp" your jars each day to prevent explosive accidents. Just a little release of the pressure each day will do the trick.

(To identify an experienced fermenter, check the ceiling of their kitchen. The telltale sign is that you'll notice a colorful splattering of fruit, vegetables and juices stuck to the ceiling!)

DAY TWENTY – What's up, Doc?
Carrot salad (almost) just like my mama's

This is one of my favorite recipes! You can serve it as a salad dish alongside just about any main dish because it's juicy and crunchy and loaded with flavors.

It's a recipe that my mom inspired me to make. When I was a kid, she'd grate up carrots, chop in some pineapple or apples or oranges, toss it all with raisins and stick it together with a dollop of mayo and a sprinkle of sugar. Sometimes she'd chop some pecans in there too.

It was like having a dessert with dinner.

Taking the same basic ingredients and fermenting them adds a tanginess you're going to grow to love. So let's make us some carrot salad with a kick of probiotics.

I'll give you the basics and you can adjust according to your own tastes.

Ingredients:

- 4 or 5 big, chunky carrots, grated
- a handful of chopped pineapple chunks (you can get them in the frozen section of your market if you need a short cut)
- one apple, any kind, diced or cut into "matchsticks"
- a handful of raisins – make sure there are no added sulfites, oils or other ingredients
- 1 tablespoon of grated fresh ginger
- juice and zest of a half lemon
- water if needed
- 1 or 2 teaspoons non-iodized salt – taste as you go so it won't be too salty
- a squeeze of honey, maple syrup, brown sugar or other natural sweetener.

Other possible ingredients:

- You can switch out the lemon for an orange.
- You can leave out the pineapple or apple.
- You may sprinkle in some spices like cinnamon, cloves, turmeric, star anise.
- Chopped pecans add a lovely crunch.

Tools:

- grater
- measuring spoons
- zester (like an itty bitty grater)
- bowl
- knife
- cutting board
- jar with lid
- canning funnel to keep things neat and tidy if you're that kind of person
- tamping tool or small baseball bat – your choice, Sport

The Process:

1. Put all your ingredients into the bowl. Wait about 30 minutes for the salt to draw the juice out of the veggies and fruits. If you like orange stain under your fingernails, be sure to massage the carrots after 30 minutes. Or not.

2. Tamp or otherwise shove the carrot mixture into your quart jar a bit at a time, pressing down to extract juices. When you're an inch or two from the top, stop. If you have leftover carrot salad, stir in a little mayo and eat it for a snack.

3. If there's not enough juice, you can pour in a little water to top it off.

4. You can slice some lemons as a follower to lay across the top of your carrot salad in the jar if you'd like to keep the bits from floating above the brine. Or use something else. Add a weight on top to keep all your ingredients submerged.

5. Affix your lid. And put your jar into hibernation for a day or so. If your lid has an airlock, leave it to do its air-releasing magic. If you have a tight lid, be sure to burp your baby each day as the gasses build up.

6. Taste your carrot salad occasionally to see if it's got the tanginess you desire. When it tastes just right to you, move it to the refrigerator.

To eat...

You can serve this carrot salad on the side as-is with just about any type of dish. If you want to stir in some mayo, be sure to drain the carrots first. Or use them straight to top off a green salad. The carrots are tangy, so I'd just say toss the salad with a bit of olive oil and sprinkle in some of your favorite salad herbs.

I'm sure you can think of other ways to use it. It's so easy and versatile, I love making it again and again.

NOTE ON ACTIVE FERMENTS:
This SO DELICIOUS ferment had a whole lotta shakin'
goin' on – it burbled out of the airlock on top till I thought
there couldn't be any juice left.

But it was plenty juicy. I think that the combination of
carbohydrates in there just excited each other so much they
had to dance!

What a drippy mess I had in my bookcase! Why didn't I put it
in a pan to catch drippings? I don't know. Just not thinking, I
guess. Oh well. I'll remember next time… right?

DAY TWENTY ONE – Criss-cross applesauce

Did your kindergarten teacher used to say "Criss-cross applesauce" when she wanted you to sit down? That tricky little teacher technique is called "Pattern Interruption." It's supposed to interrupt the chaotic pattern the little darlings are headed in and redirect them by confusing them with a random phrase and make them open to the suggestion that you'd like them to sit down... or listen to you... or get back to the lesson.

Teachers have gotten very sophisticated with their "criss-cross applesauce" type interruptions, changing it out for high fives and animal sounds and call and response poems. But we still love our applesauce – so let's make it even more delicious and nutritious with fermentation.

My daughter's apple tree was popping out little green apples. So many that we didn't know what to do with them all. So I took some home to do a little experiment.

Ingredients:

- a dozen or more apples, depending on their size, and depending and how much applesauce you want
- brown sugar or maple syrup to taste
- salt to taste
- cinnamon or other spices to taste
- a starter, such as a splash of water kefir or whey or some juice from a fermented chutney

Tools:

- peeler
- knife
- blender
- spoon
- jars
- lids
- canning funnel

The process:

1. You may peel your apples if you like, or leave the peels on. Just be sure to remove the core. No seeds, please.

2. Chunk them up and transfer to your blender along with any flavorings you like, including sweetener, salt, spices and starter if you're using one.

3. Blend till smooth.

4. Pour into jars. Add your lid. If your lid has an airlock, leave it to do its air-releasing magic. If you have a tight lid, be sure to burp your jars each day as the gasses build up.

5. Put your applesauce into a room temperature area and allow to ferment for a couple of days.

6. Get in there with a spoon and taste it to confirm that it's up to your tanginess standards. Then refrigerate.

To eat…

Use it as you would any applesauce. Pour over pancakes/latkes. Freeze into popsicles. Serve with pork. Bake with it, replacing the oil in a recipe with applesauce. Blend it into a yogurt or milk kefir smoothie. Spread it out in a dehydrator or on parchment paper and make it into fruit leather.

I make little sealed pouches of applesauce mixed with oatmeal for our baby and toddler grandkids. But since this is fermented, I'd recommend filling the pouch right before eating, or the airtight pouch just might puff up with gasses and decorate baby's face when opened. When it's refrigerated, it doesn't stop fermenting. It just slows down. The applesauce will still be creating happy gas for you.

Just letting you know so you don't end up with sauce on your face.

Just for fun, I made fruit leather from our applesauce in a round dehydrator.

It looked like an LP (Long Play/big record) when it came out. With scissors I cut around and around to make it into strips.

What good is fruit leather if you can't play with it?

DAY TWENTY TWO – Pickled in kvass.
Or, why are my eggs pink?

On Day Sixteen we put some diced beets in some saltwater and (after waiting) came up with a drink that is both "earthy" and "heavenly." That would be beet kvass.

Now if I know my readers, and I'm sure I do, you were most likely thinking, "If only I could make some pink eggs out of this kvass…"

Since that's certainly what you're thinking, let's do it!

Why do I want pink eggs?

The product of soaking hard-boiled eggs in beet kvass isn't just a pink egg. But if it were, it would still be awesome.

I'd like to suggest that you can add a kick of flavor to your hard-boiled eggs at the same time you're turning them pink.

Ingredients:

- 12 hard-boiled eggs
- several cups of beet kvass
- a cup of juice (aka "gut shots") from another vegetable ferment you like the flavor of such as sauerkraut, mixed veggies, kimchi, pickle juice or other.
- small onion, sliced
- seasonings you enjoy such as garlic, dill, coriander, rosemary… your ferment, your choice

Process:

1. Cook, cool and peel your eggs. (I use my Instant Pot for perfect eggs every time.)

2. Place eggs and seasonings in a half gallon jar

3. Pour in beet kvass plus gut shots from previously fermented veggies

4. Put a lid on it and store it in the refrigerator until your eggs have taken on color and the flavors. I left mine in overnight, and that turned them a deep magenta.

5. Strain out the eggs and onions. You can keep the beet kvass to drink or otherwise enjoy.

How to eat them:

These guys look so dramatic in a deviled egg dish.

Slice them into a chef's salad.

Chop them into egg sandwiches.

Cut in half, arrange them on a plate with a fermented hummus, bean or ranch dip.

NOTE ABOUT LABELING YOUR JARS:
Do you find it hard to remember what you've put in your jar and when you first closed the lid? Here are a few shared ideas:

- *Make notes on a calendar.*
- *Stick a piece of masking tape on your jar with the information.*
- *Use sticky notes.*
- *Write directly on your jar with a "glass pen" (with chalk ink) – it washes off easily in water.*

DAY TWENTY THREE – So you think you're a fermenting fail? Q & A

If you've gotten this far, you probably have questions.

And I've got answers. But my answers may not answer your questions. Because a lot of the time the answer is… "sometimes"… "maybe"… "depends"… and "your ferment, your choice."

But the best answer will always be: don't give up, try again.

In this chapter, I'm going to share some of the most frequently asked questions that I'm aware of. You just might find something in here that you were wondering about.

QUESTIONS ABOUT SAUERKRAUT AND KIMCHI

Q: My sauerkraut came out too salty. What can I do?
A: You can rinse your sauerkraut by soaking it first in some cool water, then drain and rinse a second time. Next time you make sauerkraut, stir in less salt than you think you need and taste it before you even pack it into your jar. If it's not salty enough, sprinkle in some more. Just keep adding salt until it tastes good to you. It's easier to add salt rather than take it out.

Q: How often should I be tasting my sauerkraut as it ferments?
A: You can open up your vessel and take some out any time you like. You're tasting for the tanginess that tells you it's fermenting. Your ferment will go through a few stages of development. You might like to eat some after five days. If you want it to go longer, push all your veggies under the brine, put the weight or follower back on if you have one, and put a lid on it. Come back after another week and taste again. Each time, be sure to push the ferment back down under the brine and secure it there.

Q: What if my cabbage doesn't make enough brine?
A: It could happen. You might not have the freshest cabbage in the patch. Although you sliced it very thin, salted it, waited for the juice to be pulled out by osmosis, massaged your shreds and tamped everything down tightly, there's just not enough natural juice to cover. In that case, make some brine out of water and salt and pour just enough into your jar to submerge your veggies. Something I like to do to encourage juiciness is to include something in my sauerkraut like apples or grated carrots.

Q: There was plenty of liquid when I started my sauerkraut, but now there are pockets of space. Do I need to take action?
A: Maybe. During the fermenting process, there comes a time when your cabbage will re-absorb some of the liquid. It's still there. You just can't see it because it's been absorbed. It's not recommended to add more brine after your sauerkraut is actively fermenting. A simple suggestion is to open your jar, push down on the cabbage and it should go back

under the brine. If there still isn't enough liquid, pull out some of the dry cabbage on top and push the rest down.

Q: I packed my jars too full and the brine is coming out the top. What should I do?
A: I've done this too. I'd rather have too much brine flowing out the top than not enough brine. That's why we set our jars in a bowl or tray. (Because when we forget we just might find gobs of carrot juice leaking out from the fermenting shelf and puddling up on the floor and seeping into a pile of laundry. Just saying it might happen to someone out there somewhere at some time.)

Q: When I opened my sauerkraut it smelled "off" and I wasn't inclined to take a chance in eating it. It looked like it had a growth of some kind on it. I tried adding more cabbage, but it still smelled rotten.
A: Believe your nose – it knows! Feed it to the garbage pail, scrub out your vessel and start fresh. The reason you shouldn't add more cabbage or brine after 24 hours is because your ferments go through various stages as they mature. When you introduce a new ingredient after the party's started, it's going to throw off the acidic balance.

QUESTIONS ABOUT FERMENTING VEGGIES IN GENERAL

Q: I've heard that if my fermented veggies are too salty, I should just wait and it will get less salty. Is this true?
A: Yes… and no.
If it's sauerkraut mainly made from cabbage, the answer is no. It will not become less salty over time. Sauerkraut is "dry brined." That means you've extracted the juice of the cabbage to use as the brining liquid without adding more water. The saltiness of the brine is already mixed with the juice of the vegetable when you put it into your jar. It is not going to get more dilute. The saltiness you taste now when you put it into your jar or crock is the saltiness that you'll taste later. That's why we say "salt to taste" when you're making a dry brine like sauerkraut.
If you're fermenting whole veggies, like cucumbers (pickles), you're plunking your big fat juicy whole veggies into a brine made from water and salt. As your veggies hang out in that salty water, osmosis draws juice out of the veggies that mixes with the salty water. Osmosis is the process where molecules pass through the semi-permeable membrane of the veggie (the peel) to try and equalize the concentration of the solids and liquid on each side of it. So the veggie juice flows out into the more-concentrated salt solution, and they mix. Then the equalized, diluted solution flows back into your veggies to make them into sour pickles. What started out as a 5% solution of salt may end up mixing with enough vegetable juice to dilute it to a 3% or less solution of salt.

Q: Is it possible to ferment without salt?
A: Yes, it's possible. I've made sauerkraut without salt. It tasted bland on its own, but it was good stuffed in an omelet and sprinkled on a pizza – both of which have lots of flavors on their own. Salt is traditionally used to draw out juice from the cabbage and discourage harmful bacteria from the get-go so that the good bacteria can take over. If you don't use salt you might want to give your ferment a kick start by using something

like 2 tablespoons of brine with live bacteria from a previous ferment. But you don't have to. Your ferment, your choice.

Q: Where do you get whey?
A: Whey is the yellowish clear liquid that you get when you drain yogurt of milk kefir. It is not the same as powdered whey.

Q: I've just finished making fermented green beans. Can I reuse the liquid and spices to make a new batch?
A: The liquid at the end of a batch of fermented food doesn't have the right balance of bacteria to start a new ferment from scratch. That's not to say you should throw it out. You can use a couple of tablespoons of it to kick start a new ferment. And as for the rest of the liquid, bottle it up and drink it – it's sold in the stores as "Gut Shots." Probiotics abound in the liquid of a finished ferment.

Q: I've heard that green beans have a high risk of botulism when you can them. Is botulism a risk when fermenting foods?
A: Fermenting is a way to guarantee NO botulism can survive in your vegetables. Although botulism can develop when food is improperly canned at home, lacto-fermentation acidifies your food, a condition that botulism can't thrive in.

Q: Is using vinegar in ferments harmful to the ferment?
A: Sometimes it is. Vinegar kills certain bacteria. But if your recipe specifically calls for using vinegar, I won't argue.

Q: I'm noticing that the liquid in my fermenting jars looks a bit cloudy, and it's foaming at the top. Is this good?
A: Cloudy brine and bubbles are signs of life.

Q: Can I use dried herbs in my vegetable ferments, or are only fresh herbs acceptable?
A: It's fine to use dried herbs. With all the moisture gone, though, you'll need to measure smaller amounts than if you were using fresh herbs.

Q: What should I do with my ferments when it's time to put them in the refrigerator?
A: If you're using an airlock lid, change it out for a regular lid so that you can use it again. Take out the weight and follower, and put your jar in the refrigerator, brine and all. Even if it looks dry, it's not.

Q: Can I reuse the brine from a finished ferment to make another batch of fermented vegetables?
A: The only re-use for a brine is when you want to add just a tablespoon to encourage a new ferment to start up quickly. But the fermenting vegetables need to go through a process

QUESTIONS ABOUT FERMENTING FRUIT

Q: Can berries be fermented?
A: Yes. Any berries are good for lacto-fermentation except strawberries, which are too acidic. But strawberries can be used to create lots of carbonation in water kefir and kombucha. ("Look out, they spit!")

Q: Should I wash my fruits and veggies before fermentation?
A: Rinse off all visible signs of dirt. Cut away any parts that are mushy or look funky. Don't sterilize them with hydrogen peroxide wash like they sell in the produce section of some stores. That stuff will kill off the good bacteria that are needed for fermentation. And while we're talking about it, don't buy irradiated food either, for the same reason.

Q: Can I substitute stevia or artificial sweeteners for sugar in ferments?
A: If the recipe calls for sugar, it's probably because the fruit needs carbohydrates to ferment. Artificial sweeteners and stevia powder won't give it the power it needs to do the job.

Q: Can I make tepache drinks with other fruits? (Recipe provided on Day Thirty-Four)
A: Some yes. Others don't taste very good. Experiment to see what you like. The basic recipe is to cut up fruit (including the rind or peel) into large chunks and put them in a clean half-gallon sized jar. Use your tamper to muddle the fruit just a bit to extract a little juice. Dissolve a scant half cup or less of sucanat or sugar in a cup of warm water. Add cinnamon or other seasonings as desired. Add cool water and fill the jar of fruit to within an inch of the top. Screw on a lid and wait anywhere from one to four days, tasting as you go. BONUS: You can re-use the fruit for another batch after straining off your liquid. Add in a little back-slosh from the previous tepache when you reuse the fruit.

QUESTIONS ABOUT LIQUID FERMENTS

Q: Since tepache (recipe provided on Day Thirty-Four) is made with the rind of fruit, I'm curious about the safety issue. How do you clean the rind well enough?
A: When you're using the skins of anything, remember that some farms spray fruits and vegetables with chemicals, in which case it will be absorbed into the skins. I'd suggest buying ingredients that are certified organic, or from a trusted farmer. If that's not possible, wash your produce in a veggie wash made with apple cider vinegar and water.

Q: My beet kvass keeps getting moldy before I can drink it. What am I doing wrong?
A: Beets are very nutritious, and that's why things grow on them. Make sure your beets are fresh and clean. Keep the beets under the brine as they ferment. And agitate your kvass by giving it a swirl now and then. If some renegade mold spores happened to land

in your jar, when you break up the surface of the kvass with a quick stir/swirl, they get overcome by the good bacteria below. It will be as if they never even came along. Become an agitator. Do it daily if you can.

Q: My friend's kombucha is fizzier than my kombucha. Why?
A: This is known as fizz envy. Are you doing a second ferment? If so, are you bottling your kombucha when it is still a little sweet? It needs sweetness to make the carbonation. Are you adding some carbohydrate-rich fruit to your second ferment for the kombucha to consume? Try that. Is your friend's house warmer than your house? Warmth helps develop bubbles. Lastly, are your bottles air tight? Seal them up well to keep the gasses in the kombucha.

Q: Can I use an airlock lid to ferment my water kefir and kombucha?
A: Water kefir and kombucha need air to ferment. Top your jars with a cloth or paper coffee filter secured with a rubber band.

Q: There's some kind of sediment in my kombucha. Should I throw it out?
A: The sediment in kombucha and water kefir is harmless. Often what you're seeing is a new SCOBY growing or some yeast. If it bothers you, just filter it out.

Q: Do I have to keep making water kefir every 48 hours? I'll have way too much if I do that!
A: There's no harm in making a batch, then storing your grains in fresh sugar water in the refrigerator for a few days until you want to make some more.

DAY TWENTY-FOUR – Hot chili sauce.
or, fire in the hole!

Over the next few days of fermenting, I've got some condiments for you to consider, starting with hot chili sauce.

WARNING * WARNING * WARNING

<u>The potential pain inflicted by chili peppers are not to be underestimated.</u>
<u>Do not allow children to handle peppers or breathe the fumes.</u>

Capsaicin is the compound in chilies that burns your mouth, skin, eyes and lungs. So why does my friend, I'll call him "Joe," love spicy foods and come back for more? Why does "Joe" like to feel the burn? Psychologists call it *benign masochism.* That means that my friend likes to take a walk on the wild side, enjoying something punishingly painful, knowing there's no real danger involved. Just PAIN.

So let's make some "Fire in the Hole" chili sauce for our benignly masochistic friends who like to feel the burn.

Ingredients:

- several peppers of your choice
- a sweet red pepper
- 1 unpeeled carrot
- half of an onion
- several cloves of garlic
- herbs you may enjoy include cardamom and Italian herbs of your choice
- salted water – approximately one teaspoon salt per cup of water

NOTE: AGAIN… WARNING: As you chop and de-seed your hot chilies, beware of breathing the fumes. It really will hurt your throat. Open a window and keep the chilies away from your face. I urge you to wear protective gloves while you handle the chilies. The capsaicin will stay on your fingernails and skin. You may feel itching and burning. Later, you might touch your eye, nose or lips and feel itching and burning.

Process:

1. Dissolve salt in water. It helps to warm some water first, dissolve salt, and then cool to room temperature.

2. Wearing gloves, chop all your vegetables, and de-seed your chilies.

3. Move all your vegetables to a jar. Tamp them down with a tamper. Pour in salted water to an inch below the top.

4. Place a weight on your vegetables to keep them submerged.

5. Close the jar.

6. Place your jar on a dish to catch the liquid as it bubbles out during fermentation.

7. Let them ferment in your fermentation station at room temperature for 5 days to a week or even several weeks. Remember to "burp" out the gas daily by loosening and then tightening the lid back on. Check to make sure that all the vegetables are staying below the brine.

> *NOTE: I like to be an agitator when it comes to fermenting.*
> *What I mean by that is that I like to give my fermenting fruits and veggies a bit of a swirl now and then. I believe that if there is some mold or yeast that's trying to settle on the surface of your ferment, breaking up their party with a swirl lets the natural lacto-fermentation do its job in chasing off anything that doesn't belong there.*

8. When your chilies are fermented to your liking, carefully drain them through a sieve, saving the brine in a separate bowl. The brine can be used as a condiment, added to marinades, sprinkled on foods at the table, added to deviled eggs, etc.

9. Place the drained vegetables in a blender. Add enough brine to liquefy the vegetables. If you like your hot sauce sweet, sprinkle in a spoon of sugar. If you like it vinegary, you can add a splash of that. Your ferment, your choice.

10. Add just a dribble of brine at a time as you blend to desired consistency. It's better to add just a little at a time, because you can't take it out once it's in. Blend until it pours the way you want it to pour.

11. Transfer your hot sauce into small glass bottles with a narrow neck, small jars, or squeeze bottles. Refrigerate.

12. Flavors will continue to develop as your hot sauce matures. Use at any time – or just give it to my friend Joe. With him, the hotter the better.

What 'cha gonna do with your fire in the hole sauce?

- Bloody Mary (see recipe in Day Thirty-Five)
- Buffalo cauliflower and other vegetables
- Buffalo wings
- Burritos
- Cajun recipes
- Chili
- Chili Rellenos
- Chutney
- Dips, stirred into kefir cheese, dripped yogurt or sour cream
- Fondue
- Fruit salad, ole
- Hamburgers and other ground meats
- Meat marinades
- Pickle-ada (see recipe in Day Thirty-Five)
- Mustard – add it to the soaking liquid for extra hot mustard
- Pasta sauce comes alive with it
- Pizza
- Popcorn
- Potatoes (Sprinkled on pan-fried potatoes or French fries)
- Ribs
- Rice
- Salad dressings, like fired up Thousand Island
- Sandwich
- Stir fry
- Tacos
- Tartar sauce

DAY TWENTY-FIVE – Hurry up, ketchup

Who came up with the word, "ketchup"?

My sources (Internet search) tell me it's an old Chinese word meaning the brine of pickled shellfish. In other words, fermented fish sauce.

Down through time, the word "ketchup" became a catch-all term for a variety of sauces made not only from fish guts, but in some cases from walnuts. Or peaches. Or lemons. Or plums… etc.

But ketchup was not a sauce made from tomatoes until the early 1800's. That's because people believed tomatoes were deadly… which is true if you were to eat large quantities of the leaves and unripe fruit.

These days, people of all ages enjoy slathering tomato ketchup on hot dogs, burgers, fish and chips and French fries. You've probably heard stories of people who slather it on a whole lot of other foods too – some rather inappropriately to some people's tastes. But they enjoy it all the same.

> *NOTE: "Ketchup" and "catsup" are alternate spellings for the same product. "Ketchup" is used more often, though. My theory for this spelling's popularity is that it is more fun to eat things that begin with a "K."*

With the following recipe, you can make flavorful fermented tomato ketchup. Use this recipe as a starting point, then experiment with other seasonings as you mix your own cultured condiments.

Ingredients:

- 24 oz. tomato paste
- ¼ cup Worcestershire sauce
- ¼ cup honey or maple syrup or brown sugar
- ¼ cup whey or water kefir or liquid from previous ferment
- ¼ cup water
- ¼ cup apple cider vinegar
- ¼ teaspoon each cinnamon, cloves, white pepper, smoked paprika, onion powder, garlic
- 2 teaspoons non-iodized salt

Process: Mix all the ingredients together. Pour into a quart jar. Screw on a tight lid and let it ferment at room temperature for 2 or 3 days, burping the lid daily. Move your jar to the refrigerator for 3 more days before eating.

FUN PROJECT: Ask kids what they like to eat ketchup on... you might be surprised!

Write answers here:

_____

_____

_____

_____

DAY TWENTY-SIX – Mayo clinic

I'm shocked at the price of good mayonnaise. You know what I mean. The kind that has a short list of ingredients that doesn't include soybean oil, preservatives or "natural flavorings" – whatever that is!

I'm also shocked at how quickly I can whip up a jar of mayo out of ingredients I have at home.

Sadly, the creamy, delicious, healthy, inexpensive mayo we make at home has a rather short shelf life… UNLESS you ferment it! Follow the instructions below, measuring carefully and doing everything in the order as listed for the best results.

> *NOTE ON THE VALUE OF EXPERIENCE:*
> *I've made a lot of mayonnaise successfully. I've also made it unsuccessfully and tried to hide it from my family.*
> *Successful mayonnaise is thick, creamy and fresh tasting.*
> *Unsuccessful mayonnaise looks like chunks of partially coagulated curds of some sort floating in slime. The best way to hide your failure is to pour it into a ziplock bag, seal it tightly, and carry it to the outside garbage by night after everyone has gone to sleep. Don't worry, the raccoons that raid your trash won't eat it either.*

The handiest hint I ever got for making mayonnaise was, "Honey, what are you doing messing with that blender? Just use a stick blender in a jar and there ya go."

The second handiest hint was to use all the ingredients at room temperature if you want them to play well together. That way the cold things (eggs and lemon juice) don't shock the warmer things (oil, etc.) into solidifying before they are emulsified.

If you don't have a stick blender, then your upright blender will work. It's just an extra step to scrape the mayo out of the blender and into a jar when you're done.

Ingredients:

- 3 raw egg yolks (I have trouble digesting raw egg whites, so I separate my eggs)
- 1 tablespoon of fresh squeezed lemon juice
- 2 tablespoons of raw, unfiltered apple cider vinegar
- one fourth teaspoon non-iodized salt
- 1 teaspoon of dry mustard
- 1 cup of fresh, recently-opened mild tasting oil, like avocado oil or "light-taste" olive oil
- 1 tablespoon of live, active liquid whey from yogurt or milk kefir, or some live brine from a previously fermented vegetable like sauerkraut.

Process:

1. In a quart-sized wide-mouth jar add the room temperature egg yolks, lemon juice, apple cider vinegar, salt, and mustard.
2. Blend them together with a stick blender.
3. With your blender running, begin to drizzle in the oil in the thinnest stream you can possibly manage. If you have a funnel or a squeeze bottle with a little tip on it, it makes it easier to add your oil in a thin stream.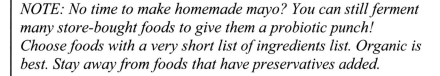
4. Keep blending until the oil stops emulsifying and it starts to puddle on the top. Even if you haven't used up the full cup of oil, stop.
5. Blend in your whey, or live brine from a previously fermented food. This is the part that is key to making your mayo last a long time and stay fresh.
6. Screw on a tight lid and let your mayonnaise sit at room temperature out of direct sunlight for 8 hours.
7. Move it to the refrigerator where it will thicken overnight.
8. For best flavor, use it within 2 weeks of making it.

DAY TWENTY-SEVEN – Mustard that bites, nips, growls and whimpers

Have you ever wished that you could have everything your way?

Well, you can't. That's what studying the inner workings of our good bacteria tells us. They need each other to survive as a whole, and so do we. Give and take. Hunger and fullness. Smooth sailing and stormy seas.

But as of now, you CAN have mustard the way you like it. And isn't that something?

When you take a bite of mustard, do you like it to bite back? Or do you just want it to have a flavor that says, "I am mustard, hear me roar" or growl or whimper?

Have it your way

By mixing different colors of seeds – black, brown and yellow – you'll give your mustard the vocalization you're looking for in a condiment.

> *NOTE: Freshly blended mustard will be more potent at the start. If it tastes like some kind of a chemical weapon right out of the blender, then it's probably just right. It will mellow as it sits in the fridge.*

Ingredients and Instructions

1. Measure **three-fourths cup of mixed mustard seeds** into a quart jar. Yellow are mildest, black and brown are spiciest. Mix them as you prefer – your ferment, your choice.
2. Cover the seeds with **brine made with a scant tablespoon of ground sea salt dissolved in 2 cups of water.** Screw on the lid tightly. Some seeds may float, but that's okay.
3. Let your seeds ferment for around 5 days or more. Swirl your jar each day and burp out the gasses as needed. Seeds will expand greatly. Leave plenty of room in the jar.
4. The magic is about to begin… strain out your seeds, reserving the brine, and toss them in the blender (or use a stick blender right in the jar if you can manage it).

5. Add in the ingredients you like to taste in your favorite mustard. I like **turmeric, honey (or maple syrup) and white wine vinegar.** Splash in some of the brine if you like it a bit salty. Splash in some lemon juice if you like it a bit tart. Add water if you need to ramp up the moisture. Your mustard will grow in volume A LOT.
6. Blend to a consistency that seems good to you. Coarse or smooth.
7. Spoon mustard into jars and store it in the refrigerator for a few days to allow the flavors to blend and mellow.

Your mustard makes a delightful gift. It's delicious on meats, in sandwiches, stirred into deviled eggs and blended into salad dressings.

MUSTARD VARIATIONS

BITES: Use more brown seeds than yellow seeds when fermenting. Blend drained seeds with horseradish, apple cider vinegar or white wine vinegar, ginger, nutmeg and cinnamon.

NIPS: Use half brown seeds and half yellow seeds. Blend drained seeds with apple cider vinegar or white wine vinegar and chopped shallots or garlic.

GROWLS: For a Dijon-style mustard, ferment half brown seeds and half yellow. Next, drain and blend smooth adding white wine that has been heated to remove the alcohol.

WHIMPERS: Use mostly or all yellow seeds. After fermenting, drain the seeds. In a blender, add seeds, apple cider vinegar or white wine vinegar, honey, maple syrup or sugar.

GERMAN: What we call German mustard is made following the basic mustard recipe, then blend in honey, brown sugar, horseradish and applesauce.

BEER: For a beer-flavored mustard, add a dark ale that has been heated to evaporate the alcohol.

You're not confined to make your mustard with only these ingredients. If you want to brighten your colors up, add some powdered turmeric. To get that herbal taste, blend in your favorite dried herbs.

What did I tell you? Your mustard, your way!

DAY TWENTY-EIGHT – Pickle me
and I'll follow you anywhere

Silly me. I thought that just because you see thousands of cucumber pickles lining grocery store shelves, they must be easy to make.

They are… and they aren't. But hey – you've already taken on quite a few fermenting projects, and I think you are up to the challenge!

Most of those cucumber pickles you see are not fermented. They're just soaked in vinegar and spices and canned in jars using a heat process. Heat-canned pickles don't have the broad spectrum of microbes you're looking for in a truly fermented food. Vinegar-soaked pickles are easy to make. But they're not particularly nourishing.

Cucumbers are finicky

Fermented pickles are a much better product. They're crunchy, sour and savory. But they can be finicky. When you make fermented pickles you may run into these problems:

- soggy/ Mushy consistency
- not sour enough
- hollow
- shriveled
- weird color
- mold or yeast on top of the brine
- no flavor

It may take you a few runs at it to get your pickles to work the way you want them to. So don't give up. Just analyze and start over, trying things a little differently.

The first thing you want to do is make sure you are using the right kind of cucumbers for the kind of pickles you want. Salad cucumbers are not usually thought of as pickle cucumbers. They have thin skins, so they'll come out softer and possibly mushy.

To make the traditional kind of pickles that are sour and crunchy, look for Kirby cukes. They are thick-skinned enough to stand up to the fermenting process. They have those iconic little warts all over them that makes you say, "Now THAT'S a pickle!"

The next thing is to ensure that your cucumbers are very fresh. If you grow your own, you can put them in a brine the very day you pick them. Can't get fresher than that.

But not a lot of us have access to a garden of cukes. Next best is a farmer's market.

Size matters

How big? That's up to you. Little ones are good. Biting into a big, juicy pickle is fun too. Sometimes you just have to go with whatever you can get that's fresh.

Probably the thing you need to be most aware of when fermenting whole cucumbers is using the same size in your ferment so that they all come to maturity at the same time. If you can't get them the same size, you can always slice them all to the same thickness.

Taste matters, too. Before you pickle your cucumbers, taste one or two from the batch raw. If it's bitter now, it will most likely be bitter later.

Wash gently, pack in brine and seasonings, wait

The instructions for making traditional dill cucumbers are basically the same as fermenting most other vegetables. However, you'll be using a saltier brine.

This is because as your cucumbers ferment, they'll be releasing a lot of sweet juice into the mix. If they are big, extra juicy cucumbers, they will dilute the brine even more.

You'll also be spicing them up more than you might other ferments. Cucumbers need a lot of in-your-face spices to give them flavor.

Lastly, you'll need to babysit these finicky ferments pretty closely. Some get finished sooner than others. Taste to see how they're doing along the way.

I like to agitate the jar now and then by giving it a little swirl. Peek in to make sure your cucumbers aren't coming to the top like a breaching whale (shove them below the brine), and that there's nothing growing on the surface (scrape it all off and if necessary, shove your pickles back below the brine). It helps to use a good follower to hold them down, and a weight.

Ingredients:

Pickling cucumbers like Kirbys, enough to fill your crock or jar
5% brine, enough to fill the crock or jar after the spices and cucumbers are added
Spices, enough to give lots of flavor to your pickles (see suggestions below)

Process:

Make a 5% brine by dissolving 50 grams of salt into one liter of non-chlorinated water (one liter of water equals 1,000 grams). It's best to weigh your salt. But if you can't weigh it, the approximate volume of salt would be 3 level tablespoons of ground non-iodized salt to a liter or quart of water. That should get you close to a 5% solution.

Salt dissolves best in warm water. If you use warm water, let it cool to room temperature before pouring the brine over your cucumbers. Heat kills the microbes present on the cucumbers that are needed for fermentation to happen, so keep your cucumbers away from hot liquid.

Wash your cucumbers gently, rubbing off the sharp spikes if there are some. Try not to bruise the cucumber or break the peel. Pay careful attention to removing the blossom end of the cuke. Rub or slice off all bits of the blossom. No blossom bits should remain. Blossom bits = bad pickles.

Add the pickling spices to the crock, jar or bowl.

Below are a few suggestions for flavoring your pickles:
- garlic cloves (bruised by smashing a bit)
- dill heads (dry dill if you can't get fresh)
- dill leaves
- dill seed
- allspice
- juniper berries
- mustard seeds
- coriander seeds
- crushed red pepper flakes
- black peppercorns
- cloves
- cardamom
- ginger

After placing your spices in the vessel, add your cucumbers. Pour in your 5% brine on top of the cucumbers. Add a follower to hold the cucumbers under the brine, plus a weight to keep the follower in place. The brine should cover everything. Cover the vessel with an airlock lid or regular lid. If using a regular lid, burp your lids daily by loosening then tightening the lid to let out gasses.

Let your cucumber pickles ferment in a cool room away from sunlight.

The "art" of fermenting applies to pickles in that you'll be using your intuition to discover whether they're done or not. Watch for color changes. Smell for the development of sourness. Taste for tanginess. Bite into one now and then to test for texture. Trust your instincts to know whether your cucumbers are done in one week, two weeks or maybe even three depending on the variables of ingredients and temperature.

Some of the fixes for the most common pickle problems may include:

- **Soggy/ Mushy consistency** – Possibly too much of the blossom left on the cucumber before fermenting. Or the brine is too weak, or your cucumbers breached the surface and were exposed to the air. Your cucumbers may not have been fresh, or were fermented in too warm an environment. You can add tannin-rich grape leaves or tea leaves or bay leaves to keep them crisp.
- **Not sour enough** – You may not have let your pickles ferment long enough, or the environment is too cool. Easy fix is to let them ferment longer.
- **Hollow** – This may be out of your hands, and could just have something to do with how often the farmer watered their crops. I've had cucumbers from the same plant, picked at the same time end up with some hollow and some solid. Anyway, I don't mind hollow pickles.
- **Shriveled** – Your brine may have been too salty.
- **Weird color** – Things that can make your pickles off-color might be that you used powdered spice rather than whole spices. Your water may be too mineralized. Or you may have left them to ferment for too long.
- **Mold or yeast on top of the brine** – Mold will look fuzzy, and yeast will look white and filmy. Keep air out of your jar as much as possible to prevent these growths. Swirling the jar occasionally will release the mold-killing power of the lacto-fermentation before it gets a foothold. Make sure you have a follower and weight on your pickles so that if you do get mold, it's just a surface problem and can be scraped gently off without disturbing the pickles underneath.
- **No flavor** – Cucumbers are like some people I know who don't do well with hints and innuendo. They need you to be direct and bold with your spices.

"Good ideas, like good pickles, are crisp, enduring, and devilishly hard to make."

– Rushworth Kidder, founder of the Institute for Global Ethics

DAY TWENTY-NINE – Green Beans, the taste of pickles without the fuss of cucumber

Now that you know how difficult a cucumber can be (from Day Twenty-Eight), let's talk about the good kid in the garden. The humble green bean.

Green beans are not finicky in any way. They grow like weeds and pickle up in no time without the fuss a cucumber makes. So let's get these babies going.

You don't need anything but green beans and saltwater to make this ferment. However, if you want to dress up your humble green buddies, I've included some suggestions below.

Ingredients:
- 1 lb of fresh organic green beans (more or less)
- 2% brine – make it by stirring 15 grams salt into 3 cups of water. To measure by volume, that's about 1 tablespoon of my ground Himalayan sea salt for 3 cups of water.

To dress up your green beans, try adding any of the following:
- garlic to taste, approximately 1 clove diced
- chili pepper flakes to taste, around one half teaspoon
- juice and zest of half lemon
- chopped fresh organic ginger to taste, around 2 teaspoons
- fresh dill heads or dried dill to taste
- 1 teaspoon of whole peppercorns
- 1 bay leaf

Process:
1. Add your choice of spices to the bottom of a quart jar or a jar large enough to hold the amount of green beans you want to make.

2. Trim both ends of your green beans.

3. To fit as many beans as possible into your jar, turn it on its side and line your beans up long-ways. Stuff them in until you can't fit any more. Leave headspace at the top so you can add a follower and/or weight. If you need to snip off some ends to make them fit, you can always toss those ends in as well.

4. When all your spices and beans are packed in tightly, pour in your brine to within an inch of the top of the jar. Add a follower and/or weight to keep your beans below the brine, and still have a little room at the top.

5. Add a lid and place your beans in a room-temperature area and let them ferment for 5 to 7 days. If you don't have an airlock lid, burp your lids each day by loosening and re-tightening.

6. In a day or two, you'll see bubbles form. You may have some foaming out of your lid. Over time your brine will turn cloudy. All these events are signs of life! You're doing well, and your beany buddies will be shining stars in the end.

Every now and then, taste your beans to see if they have become tangy, or if you like the flavor. Not sour enough? Still too crunchy? Push them down back below the brine. Leave them in a few more days. When you're satisfied, remove the weight, change to a regular lid and place your beans in the refrigerator.

These now-glamorous beans are great for snacking right out of the jar, adding to a salad, or cutting up in egg, chicken or tuna salad. You can even serve them as a side with the Bloody Mary featured in Day Thirty-One.

DAY THIRTY – To-MAY-to, To-MAH-to – get your creative juices flowing!

You can find dozens of recipes telling you how to make fermented tomatoes (or toMAHtoes) in the form of whole cherry tomatoes, tomato sauce, tomato ketchup, and that's about it.

You might be luckier than I was, but I couldn't find anything I liked that told me how to make fermented tomato juice. So I set out to experiment with different ways to make it myself. Here's what finally worked…

DIY: Do It Yerself

1. Juice 3 lbs of fresh tomatoes, which makes about 1 quart of juice.

2. Add 3 teaspoons of Himalayan Pink Salt, more or less to taste.

3. (Optional) Add 2 tablespoons of starter. I used fermented pickle juice.

4. Put a lid on your jar and allow to ferment about 3 days, giving the jar a swirl a few times a day to break up any mold that may be trying to form on the surface.

5. After 3 days, move it to the refrigerator and use as you would any other tomato juice.

> *NOTE: Like most fruits, tomatoes tend to ferment and mold quickly. Adding some kind of a starter like whey or a slosh from a previously fermented vegetable will help kick lacto-fermentation into gear quickly.*

Unlike sauerkraut, tomato juice doesn't become especially tangy. It will develop a savory flavor, and a bit of fizz, thanks to lacto-fermentation.

DAY THIRTY-ONE – A curtido walks into a bar…

A curtido walks into a bar. The bartender looks up and scowls, "Sorry, we don't serve food here."

Badum-CHING.

On Day Ten you made sauerkraut. Day Fourteen introduced you to another kind of sauerkraut – one with carrots, ginger, turmeric and pineapple. Day Nineteen was all about kimchi. And today… meet curtido.

All these recipes have something in common. They're all cabbage ferments with distinctive ethnic flavors.

Curtido is a Central American fermented side dish made with cabbage, onion, carrots, and spices. You ferment it for as short as 4 days or as long as 2 weeks – depending on how sour you want it to be. Your ferment, your choice. Start tasting at 4 days, and when it's to your liking, put a lid on it and refrigerate.

Some people call it a salsa. Others, a slaw. It's delicious no matter what you call it.

Follow the same general instructions on how to make sauerkraut, using the following ingredients:

- 1 small cabbage, thinly sliced
- 2 grated carrots
- one half sweet onion, thinly sliced
- one half jalapeno de-seeded and thinly sliced (optional)
- 1 teaspoon dried pepper flakes (to your taste preference)
- juice and zest of one lime
- 1 tablespoon of dried oregano
- one half teaspoon crushed coriander (the seeds of the cilantro plant)
- one fourth teaspoon ground cumin (optional – some people don't like the taste of cumin)
- non-iodized salt to taste (about a tablespoon or more)

Putting all this in a bowl took me 15 minutes. It took that long because I had to hunt down some of the spices. They're always in the back of the cupboards! I let it sit in the bowl about a half hour while the salt drew the juice out from the vegetables.

After 30 minutes, I lit some candles, put on some soothing music, and gave it a massage. (I'm joking about the candles and music, but doesn't that sound nice?)

When it was completely relaxed, I tamped it tightly into one quart jar and one pint jar, making sure there was enough liquid to cover the top. There wasn't. So I went ahead and topped it off with a little non-chlorinated water just to bring the level up above the vegetables.

The cabbage leaf went on top as a Follower. The glass weight went on top to hold it all under the brine. I tightened down a lid and labeled my jars with the date and what was in there. And the jars went into the shelf. On a plate. To catch spills.

In 5 days I tasted it. Pretty good! Good enough to move the pint jar out of hibernation and into the refrigerator. I let the quart jar keep on fermenting about 5 more days (or until we ran out of the pint sized jar.)

This has become one of my favorite ferments. Eat alone. With chips. In tacos. On pizza. In omelets, wraps and burritos.

Curtido is perfect anytime you want to get that wonderful South-of-the-Border taste.

Ole!

DAY THIRTY-TWO – Razzle-dazzle berries

When berries are in season, they are a wonderful treat. Unfortunately, they only last about 4 to 7 days in the refrigerator in their raw state.

But if you ferment your berries, you'll be able to preserve them in your refrigerator for up to two months! Now you're talking!

Fermented berries take on a many-splendored depth of flavor and texture that you'll enjoy over yogurt, blended in smoothies, atop cheesecake, in your cereal and right out of the jar.

With all your experience over the past few weeks, I hardly need to tell you how to ferment your berries. You've got the drill down on how fermenting works. Let's sing it and swing it:

Wash up all the food, put it in the jar
Bump Bump
Pack it down real tight, sprinkle in some salt
Bump Bump
Poke some herbs in there, season it to taste
Bump Bump
Keep beneath the brine, add a little lid
Bump Bump

Then wait for it… wait for it…

You have SO got this!

Still, I'll include a few general instructions as an outline for fermenting success with berries. It's kind of my job to write it out for you, so here goes.

1. Get the freshest ripe organic berries you can find.
2. Remove stems and leaves. Wash the berries in cool non-chlorinated water.
3. Put your berries in a clean jar. Tamp them down just a little to wedge them in tightly. Leave an inch of space at the top.
4. Add seasonings. For berries, you might like to toss in star anise, allspice, or cinnamon. You might think of some other seasoning you'd like.

5. Top your berries with a follower such as a slice of lemon, or silicone disk, plus a weight. Berries like to pop up and float sometimes. But don't let them!

6. In a separate container, mix some non-chlorinated water with a tablespoon or two of honey, maple syrup, brown sugar or other organic sweetener and a little sprinkle of salt to taste, about ¼ teaspoon. Use enough water to fill your jar and cover your weight. Stir to dissolve ingredients.

7. You may want to add a starter like whey, water kefir or kombucha. (Obviously you don't want to use pickle or sauerkraut juice as a starter with fruit.) If so, add about two tablespoons of starter per pint.

8. Pour the liquid mixture into the jar of berries, making sure all the fruit is covered. Add your tight lid. Place your jar in a pan to catch drips as it may overflow when it begins to bubble. If you use an airlock lid, you can just leave your jar alone. If you use a canning type lid, be sure to burp out the gas each day.

9. They will ferment within just a couple of days, depending on the temperature of your home. Check on them, burping and swirling each day (the berries, not you…)

10. In about 2 days (or less if your house is very warm), taste your berries. They should be slightly tart and fizzy. Remove the weight, screw on a regular lid, and put your jar in the refrigerator to enjoy over the next few weeks – if you don't run out first!

By fermenting berries, you can extend the razzle-dazzle taste of the season.

DAY THIRTY-THREE – Tooty fruity

What I'm about to say may shock you.

As much as I love the savory, salty, sweet taste of fruit-based chutney, someone else might just like their fruit to taste like… well… fruit.

And it's a good thing we can successfully put everyday fruit through the process of fermenting because those gorgeous, juicy princesses of the royal Garden of Eatin' don't have a lot of staying power. I've had to toss out bag loads of ripe, fragrant peaches, plums, apricots, cherries, pineapples and more within days of bringing them home.

No more gooshy brown fruit!

Got a jar? Got some salt and water? Got a lid? Let's ferment us some fruit.

For any of the fruits I mentioned above, and several more, the process is the same.

1. Cut up your fruit and put it in a bowl.

2. Sprinkle on seasonings like cinnamon, star anise, cloves, allspice… whatever you think might be good with that fruit.

3. Sprinkle on a spoonful of sugar, because the sugar will be used to "feed" your fermentation.

4. Sprinkle on just a pinch or two of non-iodized salt.

5. Pack your fruit into a jar.

6. Pour in enough non-chlorinated water to cover your fruit, but leave at least an inch of headroom.

7. Measure in 2 tablespoons of whey for each quart of fruit you're fermenting.

8. Swirl to mix in the whey.

This next part is really important to your success

Fruit has a tendency to bob to the top of the jar. But you don't want to let it come in contact with air. So…

9. Place a follower and weight on top to hold all the fruit down. Then attach a lid to keep the liquid safe.

10. Place your jar in your fermentation station and wait.

11. Burp your jar the next day and look to make sure all the fruit is still under the liquid.

12. Wait 1 more day. Then open your jar and taste your fruit.

Here's how you'll know it's done

There will be a slight effervescence that you can feel like a fizz on your tongue. Your fruit will taste wonderfully fruity. Got fizz? Take out the weight and follower. Put a regular lid on. Put it in the refrigerator.

Eat your fruit within a few weeks – as a topping for yogurt, on cottage cheese, pancakes, oatmeal, or just on its own.

This is the tricky part about fermenting fruit

Fruit is so full of carbohydrates that it will go alcoholic on you in a single day. Don't wait too long to refrigerate it. As soon as you can feel that fermentation fizz on your tongue, move it to the refrigerator.

You don't want it to turn to alcohol. I know that sounds like fun, but the flavor suffers once your ferment has started down that road. And it can turn down that road before you can say, "One bad apple spoils the barrel."

Give fruit a chance. You may be surprised at how delightful a fermented jar of spiced pineapple, peaches or plums can be.

DAY THIRTY-FOUR – Refined rinds: making tepache

Tepache is a very popular beverage among fermenting friends. It's a drink made with fruit rinds – not the "meat" of the fruit – and presents endless potential to experiment with different flavors.

Learn by first making a pineapple tepache. And when you get that one mastered, try other fruit rinds and spices.

Ingredients:

- rind of one pineapple
- one half cup of brown sugar
- one fourth teaspoon cinnamon
- one fourth teaspoon red pepper flakes
- 6 allspice pods
- water to fill jar

Process:

1. Cut up a pineapple rind with ¼ inch to ½ inch of fruit left intact. Cut it in pieces and fit the pieces into a half-gallon jar.
2. Dissolve one half cup of sugar in warm water and allow to cool.
3. Pour the sugar water into the jar with the pineapple rinds.
4. Add the spices.
5. Add enough non-chlorinated water to fill the jar to an inch below the top.
6. Put a weight on top of the rinds to hold them securely under the liquid.
7. Cover the jar with a cloth or paper coffee filter and rubber band.
8. Ferment for 1 to 5 days, swirling and tasting as you go until you like the flavor.
9. Strain the liquid out of the jar and pour it into sealable bottles like flip-top bottles or juice bottles with a tight lid.
10. Allow the liquid to carbonate for about 3 days, burping the bottles each day until it reaches the fizziness you like.
11. Transfer carbonated tepache to the refrigerator and enjoy!

Spices to try in making your tepache:
- lemon/lime
- cinnamon sticks
- allspice
- star anise
- cardamom
- ginger
- black peppercorns
- chili peppers
- maple syrup

DAY THIRTY-FIVE – You had me at "sangria" (must be over 21)

If you are not over 21 (and I'm pretty sure you know who you are) let it be known that you must skip this chapter. It involves making and drinking alcoholic beverages. Consider yourself warned.

To enjoy these drinks, you don't need to make your own water kefir or kombucha if they're sold in your grocery store. KeVita is a brand that I've found in many local stores that makes a tasty water kefir. And our favorite store-bought kombucha is G.T.'s.

For those who imbibe… or don't

At the end of a busy day, sometimes you'd like to have more than just a little kvass to sip on. So let's get adult here… Here are some of my favorite adult beverage drinks that are also probiotic. Drink responsibly, remembering that too much of a good thing can go terribly wrong.

You can always make these fancy cocktails minus the alcohol. For the Sangria, use a grape-flavored water kefir in place of the soft red wine and you'll have a kid-friendly drink to share with the little guys.

Simple and Flavored Syrups

Some sweet drinks call for simple or flavored syrups. You can buy a bottle at most grocery stores or a liquor store. But since they really are simple, you can make them yourself and save a bundle of moola. Here's how:

BASIC SIMPLE SYRUP
Combine 1 cup boiling water with 1 cup of sugar. Stir to dissolve sugar. Let it cool.

GINGER SYRUP
Peel about a 4-inch knob of ginger – use a spoon for easy peeling; it really works! Chop ginger roughly. Combine 1 cup boiling water with 1 cup of sugar and the chopped, peeled ginger. Steep for 30 minutes. Strain and let it cool.

COCONUT SYRUP
Combine 1 cup of boiling water with 1 cup of sugar and a half cup of coconut flakes. Steep for one hour. Strain and let it cool. When completely cool, the coconut oil will float to the top. Strain one more time to remove the solidified oil.

Drink Recipes

SUPERFOOD SANGRIA
Mix in a container that you can cover:

- 1 liter of soft red wine like Lambrusco
- 2 cups of chopped fruits such as blueberries, strawberries, peaches, pears, apples
- slices of limes and oranges

Cover and let the wine steep for several hours or overnight in the refrigerator to infuse flavors.

When your wine has absorbed the flavors of the fruits, pour it all into a pitcher with ice and add:

- one half cup of brandy
- 1 cup of bubbly orange water kefir (or fizzy orange whey drink)
- 1 cup of bubbly grape water kefir
- 1 cup of peach, apple or pineapple water kefir
- Sweeten with sugar or simple syrup if you prefer a sweeter Sangria.
- Serve over ice with a slice of orange.

For a lighter, more citrus-like flavor, use white wine in place of red, and lemon kefir in place of peach, apple or pineapple.

CARA-BOOCH
Our daughter, Cara, came up with this kombucha-based drink. We really enjoyed sipping it over ice as the kids played in the sandbox with Grandpa.

Mix:
3 oz bourbon
4 oz kombucha
1 oz lime juice
1 oz simple syrup
2 tablespoons ginger syrup

Shake together and serve over ice.

BEET KVODKA

3 oz apple kefir (or your favorite flavor KeVita)
2 oz beet kvass
1 and a half oz (one shot) vodka
1 tablespoon ginger syrup
1 teaspoon lime juice

Mix and serve over crushed ice.

COWBOY JOE

6 oz bubbly lemon water kefir, citrus whey drink or a store-bought water kefir drink like that made by the KeVita brand
1 oz simple syrup
1 oz fresh squeezed lime juice
3 oz (two shots) tequila
1 teaspoon orange extract or orange liqueur
Ice

Stir together ingredients. Pour over ice. Sip slowly and sway rhythmically while singing cowboy songs like "Ragtime Cowboy Joe" accompanied by Alvin and the Chipmunks. Or any of the old favorites like "Home, Home On The Range" and "Down In The Valley."

That'll make it a party you won't forget, unless you have several Cowboy Joe drinks, that is. Drink responsibly so you can remember the fun.

PINA-KEF-OLADA SMOOTHIE
(serves two)
8 oz milk kefir
2 tablespoons coconut syrup or ½ cup sweetened cream of coconut
(If you can't get cream of coconut, just use coconut cream sweetened with your favorite sweetener)

8 oz pineapple juice, or juice from your pineapple ferment
one half cup frozen pineapple tidbits (Trader Joe's has this)
Several ice cubes
3 oz rum
Whipped cream
Cherry, fermented or otherwise

Process chilled ingredients in a blender until smooth.
Pour into 2 tall, chilled glasses.
Squirt on whipped cream.
Top with a cherry (skewered on a little umbrella, if you like)
Serve with a straw for slow sipping.

Kids like this drink too, minus the rum!

BLOODY MARY

In the photo below, one of these drinks is with vodka and one without – can you tell which is which?

Ingredients:
- 3 oz fermented tomato juice
- hot sauce to taste
- dash of Worcestershire sauce
- lemon and lime juice to taste
- 1 shot of vodka

Combine all ingredients in a small jar. Garnish with lime and stir with a celery stick. In my house, we call this "salad."

PICKLE-ADA

1. Mix ½ teaspoon of chili powder with ¼ cup of salt. Rub a lime on the rim of a glass, and dip into the chili-salt mixture to coat the edge on one side.

2. Mix in the bottom of a tall glass:
- 2 tablespoons pickle juice
- 1 teaspoon Worcestershire sauce
- juice of 1 whole lime (the lime really makes this drink, so be generous!)
- 1 teaspoon hot sauce like Frank's or your own homemade pepper sauce

Add ice and slowly pour in one bottle of light golden Mexican beer.

ARNI'S LEMON TEA SIPPER
Ingredients:

- one half cup of strong tea – black, oolong or hibiscus
- 1 cup of fizzy lemon based water kefir or KeVita
- 1 tablespoon of ginger syrup
- 1 shot of vodka or other clear spirit
- Ice
- Sprig of mint

Combine in a glass filled with ice and enjoy sipping this refreshing beverage after a day of yard work or sports. But take off your shoes before coming in to put your feet up.

TEPACHE NIGHTCAP
 with whiskey and splash of angostura bitters

On Day Thirty-Four you made a tepache with pineapple rinds. Now put it together with a splash of bourbon whiskey and call it a night (cap).

Pour into a pint jar filled with ice:

8 ounces Tepache
2 ounces whiskey
1½ teaspoons Angostura Bitters

Stir and sip

DAY THIRTY-SIX – Fake sourdough

I tried. I really tried.

I bought the "San Francisco" sourdough starter. I babied it. Fed it. Kept it at the right temperature. Used all the right kinds of flour. But no. It was just not going to happen.

I thought that sourdough was not my thing. Until… FAKE SOURDOUGH!

Oh yeah! You get your bread flour. You get your salt. You get your milk kefir. And magic happens.

Here's how:

1. In a bowl, scoop in **3 cups of bread flour** (I am a fan of "King Arthur.")

2. Add around a **teaspoon of salt** to taste and mix.

3. Pour in **1½ cups of fermented milk kefir.**

4. Stir the dough, adding flour as needed to make a kneadable dough. When it is no longer sticky, pull it out of the bowl and knead it on the counter top just a bit. Once it feels smooth and you can roll it around without it sticking to anything, you're good to go.

5. Form the dough into a loaf, any shape. Place it on a piece of parchment, or in an oiled bread pan. Cover it to keep it moist and let it sit overnight and then some in a warmish spot, like a bookcase in your laundry room, for instance. It takes a long time to raise.

6. When it looks like it has doubled in size, heat the oven to around 400 degrees.

7. Pop your loaf in the oven and bake around 35 minutes, or until golden brown and done all the way through.

8. Cool your bread completely before slicing.

Best... Pizza... Dough... Ever!

Next time, you might want to flatten your dough and turn it into a pizza.

This stuff is so smooth and stretchy, I was tempted to toss it over my head and spin it around. But instead I just rolled it out. Brushed on olive oil and some of my garlic honey. Topped with leftovers and some ricotta. Sprinkled with Parmesan. And baked for about 10 minutes at 450 degrees.

What a wonderful world it is, to be able to make quick and delicious Fake Sourdough!

Now if only it were calorie-free. Well, nothing's perfect.

Speedy Tortilla

You don't even need to let the dough rise for a speedy tortilla.

Heat a pan on the cooktop to medium heat. Mix up your dough with 2 parts bread flour, one part milk kefir and salt to taste. Do a little kneading, adding enough flour as you go to get the dough un-sticky and smooth. Pull off a golf ball sized portion and roll it out on a lightly floured board or counter top. Using a rolling pin, make it as flat as you can, no bigger than the size of the pan you're cooking it in.

When the pan is hot, rub in a little oil (something that won't smoke such as avocado oil or coconut oil). Plop your flattened dough tortilla into the pan. Let it cook a few minutes, until it has a few brown spot on the underside – you'll need to peek.

Flip it over to finish cooking. At this point, you might add cheese to make a quesadilla. And why not sprinkle in something else like sauerkraut and hot pepper sauce? Fold and cool on a plate before cutting into fun-sized finger food.

DAY THIRTY-SEVEN – I don't have time for this

The nice thing about this book is that you get to try out a variety of tastes and fermenting techniques a little at a time.

As you make your way through the projects – choosing produce, chopping, salting, sloshing and eating—it will connect you more closely, hand and heart, with the food you eat. You'll begin to feel and appreciate how your food choices are contributing to your health and well-being.

Your personal experience along the way will help you decide what you enjoy making, what tastes you prefer, and which types of ferments you want to make time for.

Making the hard choice

I just don't have time to make all the homemade goodies I'd like to be eating.

For instance, although I like both yogurt and milk kefir, I only have time, energy and budget to make one or the other on a regular basis. It's the same with kombucha and water kefir. One or the other, not both.

That's not to say you can't have it all. That's just how I greet each day – with a K.I.S.S. (Keep It Simple, Sue).

Another choice I've made is to try and have sauerkraut available most of the time. So I'll take an hour to chop, massage, combine and jar up some sauerkraut. I'll make several quarts of whatever varieties sound good at the time. In a couple of weeks or a month, we can start eating from the jars, and put together a new batch for future eating.

Another fermented food I like to have on hand is the carrot salad we made on Day Twenty. That stuff dresses up the flavor and beauty of just about any meal. As a side dish on its own, it's juicy and flavorful. It's like my little jar of perpetual sunshine.

It's up to you which ferment you decide to continue making, and which ferments you need to take a break from or discontinue altogether.

Seasonal choices

The season of the year may be a factor in choosing what you'd like to ferment. In my part of the world, we can't get fresh cabbage year-round. So I need to make sauerkraut when the (cabbage) heads are rolling… like in the cooler months. Fortunately, sauerkraut keeps its deliciousness for a long, long time when stored in a cool place. Up to a year or more!

In the summer, our blackberries and blueberries are practically jumping off the bushes. Cucumbers in the garden seem to double in size every day. I'll take advantage of the abundance and low prices of various seasonal fruits as they come ripe.

You get the picture… put some ferments on hold in the off-season. And bring them back when the produce is abundant again.

Got time for three steps?

Fermenting fresh produce preserves it for much longer than if it were sitting in your refrigerator raw for weeks at a time. Did you ever discover fuzzy berries in the back of your fridge? Or a bag of cucumber mush in the produce drawer? Yeah, me neither (she lied…)

Save yourself expense and waste. It's so easy to keep produce from turning into compost. Fermenting preserves your food, adds nutrition and takes only three steps:

1. Prepare the vegetables or fruits by washing and cutting.
2. Put them into a jar with salt, water and seasonings and weigh them down so they stay under the liquid.
3. Cover and set the jar in a safe, room-temperature place away from direct sunlight. And wait.

Even though there are only three steps to most fermenting recipes, you may still need to take a break once in awhile.

Taking time away from fermenting

Most of the ferments you make end up in the refrigerator after they're done. Refrigerated, some will last for weeks, and some, like sauerkraut, can last for years!

You can stop making fermented fruits and vegetables at any time, and pick it up when you feel like you want to ferment again.

Taking a break from making kefir and kombucha is a different story. These foods include a colony of bacteria that needs to be fed as it ferments. But let's say you would really like to take a vacation. What do you do with your communities of bacteria and yeast?

Here are four ideas for taking short vacations from SCOBY-powered ferments, and a few "cool" solutions so that you can take a longer, worry-free vacation.

1. Time your short vacation

Since kombucha takes 7 to 14 days to ferment, you could start a new batch just before you leave on a trip. Make a good amount of sweet tea to feed your SCOBY. Cover it with a cloth. Put it in a safe area, away from daylight. Do not refrigerate your SCOBY. You can let it sit in a cool place while you're gone for anywhere from 1 to 3 weeks without a problem.

If you get back and discover that the kombucha tea has become too sour while you were gone, that won't matter. Your SCOBY is still healthy, even after several weeks.

You can do the same thing for water kefir if you are only going away for a short vacation. But water kefir should not be left unfed at room temperature for more than five days at the most. For longer vacations, you can refrigerate it – see the section below on "Go nighty-night."

Milk kefir normally can't be left at room temperature for more than 24 hours. If your vacation is just overnight, give your milk kefir grains a new jar of milk, and come back the next day. If you must be gone longer, add more milk. That will feed them a little longer when left at room temperature. For extended vacations, refrigerate your milk kefir as described in the section on "Go nighty-night."

2. Go nighty-night for extended vacations

When you refrigerate your milk or water kefir grains, it's like putting them into a sleep state for a short time. You'll need to prepare them by placing them in a good amount of their regular nourishing liquid and sealing the jar.

You can refrigerate your milk or water kefir grains for up to 10 days as long as they have enough nourishment to survive. I've done this several times without harming my grainy little buddies!

When you come home, strain out the liquid and give your grains a new feeding. Don't be surprised if they don't wake up right away. After all, they've been on vacation, too. It may take a couple of rounds of feeding before they can get back to work.

I've heard about people freezing their milk kefir grains when they need to leave them for more than a month. I tested it out, and it worked quite well. Here's how to freeze milk kefir grains: Put milk kefir grains in a jar of milk and placed it in the freezer. When you get home, thaw the jar of milk on the kitchen counter and then give the grains some fresh milk.

The first batch I made after freezing wasn't very thick or tasty, and I didn't expect it to be. So I strained the grains and fed them again as usual. The second batch tasted good, but was not very thick. By the third time, my grains were back to working well.

As I mentioned, kombucha SCOBYs don't do well being refrigerated. They are fair weather friends who prefer a warm climate. I know just how they feel.

3. Get a house sitter for long vacations

If you plan to hire a house sitter to stop in, water your plants, bring in the mail and check on things while you're gone, you could leave instructions for them to take care of your ferments, too. If you don't have someone coming over, you could take your ferments to a friend's house. A very good friend. And be sure to bring them a very nice thank you gift.

4. Compost and restart later

You started once, and you can do it again. Compost your SCOBY and grains. Get new ones when you come home. If you've shared your cultures with certain friends, they're likely willing to share back with you again. Let them know before you leave that you'll want to adopt some of their cultures when you get back. That will give them time to put some aside for you.

Next up on Day Thirty-Eight … exciting culinary concoctions with dairy ferments!

DAY THIRTY-EIGHT – I dairy-ya to try these recipes

What to do with your kefir cheese…

You can use your kefir cheese as a spread on crackers, mixed with herbs. Or top a baked potato in place of using sour cream. It's also delicious as a base for a creamy ranch-like salad dressing. Or just lick it off your finger when no one is looking.

Daring smoothies using yogurt and milk kefir

Build a healthy breakfast or anytime pick-me-up by combining the protein rich power of yogurt and kefir with flavors you enjoy. Here's a basic how-to to get you started on your smoothie. Once you get your stride, rev up your imagination and run with new ideas.

1. Pour milk kefir or yogurt into a blender.
2. Add some almond or coconut milk if you like.
3. Add in flavors and spices that you enjoy, plus something sweet (honey, sugar, banana etc.).
4. You can thicken up your smoothie by adding ice cubes or frozen fruits.
5. Blend until smooth.
6. Below are suggestions for combinations of flavors to consider adding to your smoothies:

    - canned pumpkin with cinnamon and cloves

- chocolate powder and instant coffee powder
- chocolate and cherries
- pineapple, cinnamon and red pepper flakes
- ginger, vanilla and orange zest
- pears, apricots, cloves, cinnamon
- cantaloupe, ginger, lemon zest, mint
- rhubarb and cardamom
- strawberry and mint
- cranberry, mango, mint
- strawberry and fresh basil leaves
- honey-fermented cranberries
- ginger and pineapple
- triple berry – blackberry, raspberry, blueberry
- ginger and lemon
- watermelon and mint
- apricot and vanilla
- loquat, pineapple and ginger
- peach with cinnamon and ginger
- pineapple, mango, papaya, coconut
- strawberries and lemon
- blueberries and lemon zest
- applesauce, ginger, cinnamon and allspice
- banana and peanut butter

Frozen desserts

Kefir cheese and yogurt also make a wonderful base for frozen desserts and popsicles. Here's an easy recipe for peanut butter iced kefir. Substitute yogurt if that's what you have on hand. Change out the flavors with chocolate, mint, caramel, pecan – anything that suits your taste.

Blend a **cup of kefir cheese**, a **cup of full-fat coconut milk**, a **cup of peanut butter**, a **cup (or less) of sugar** (or honey or other sweetener), and a **teaspoon of vanilla**. Freeze it in your ice cream maker and enjoy with a scattering of chocolate shavings on top.

You can also follow the same general recipe, and blend in an avocado instead of the peanut butter. Freeze into popsicles, dip in melted chocolate, roll in coconut and chopped nuts.

Let your imagination run wild!

DAY THIRTY-NINE – Recipes to use your fermented fruits and veggies

Sauerkraut (Day Ten):
- Put pizzazz in scrambled eggs and omelets.
- To add interest to pizza, spread some sauerkraut over the top after pulling it out of the oven.
- Stir sauerkraut into broth-based soups to add texture and tang.
- Make a casserole with Italian sausage, spicy tomato sauce and sauerkraut:
    1. In a large skillet, fry ½ pound of bacon till crispy.
    2. Add to the pan 2 fully cooked, sliced sausage links (like Aidells Italian-style chicken sausage), ½ chopped onion, 1 teaspoon of diced garlic to taste. Cook until the onion is softened.
    3. Stir in 1 cup of sauerkraut, 1 grated carrot, 1 bay leaf, 2 tablespoons of parsley, ¼ teaspoon hot pepper flakes and 1 cup of pizza sauce.
    4. Transfer to a casserole dish and top with a mix of Parmesan cheese and mozzarella.
    5. Bake in a 350 degree oven until cheese is melted.

Chutney (Day Eleven):
- Serve as an accompaniment to roasted or grilled meats.
- Use as a dip with buttered sourdough toast.
- Chutney is delish as a relish.
- The combination of sweet and tart flavors dresses up a cheese and cracker tray making it fit for royalty.

Kimchi (Day Nineteen)
- Fry up a pancake made with Korean pancake mix and kimchi.
- Top scrambled eggs or cottage cheese.

Green Beans (Day Twenty-nine)
- Using the same method, pickle okra.
- Lay green beans atop a salad with a dollop of kefir cheese.
- Pick up your beans by hand and dip them into hummus.

Curtido (Day Thirty-One)
- Slip some curtido into a taco or burrito.
- Use it to top a Mexican salad.
- Add to a burger or hot dog.

DAY FORTY – Welcome to the Potluck

By Day Forty, you'll be an expert fermenting artist. By your own hand and the grace of God's bountiful bacterial world, you will have chopped, liquefied, cultured, squeezed, mixed and sloshed your way to enhancing and preserving your food's nutrition and taste.

You'll know what you like and understand how to use it in your daily meals.

Some people love the drinking life, the sour life, the saucy life. By this time, layers of flavors have tickled your tongue. Thanks to your adventurous journey to discover new tastes, you've failed and succeeded your way toward a broadened aptitude for food and flair in the kitchen.

Better health is worth sharing

Over the past month or so, you have become more acquainted with how your body responds to fermented foods. At first, you may have experienced a bit of a purge. (Ahem… you know what I mean.) Following the purge, you may have felt a boost in your energy level.

Along with that purge and boost, the next few months may have you saying something along the lines of, "Wait a minute – I haven't had a cold for a long time. I'm not bloated or puffy-eyed each morning. I think I'm feeling rather 'regular,' and that's a good thing."

I invite you to consider opening up an opportunity to share your wealth of health with family, friends and neighbors by calling them to join you in a potluck.

Your potluck is the opposite of the perfect picnic or impeccable dinner party. This can be the most relaxing gathering of cooks and eaters you can hope for. A time to relax and let the randomness flow.

Think of a potluck as an outer expression of our inner world. A variety of talents coming together to nourish the whole. Bob brings his home baked bread. Josh bottles up some juice. Pablo tosses a salad. Chong cooks up her spicy chicken. Fabio specializes in fruit plates. And Rose roasts up a batch of her potato harvest.

And you? You'll just choose some of your favorite ferments to add to the party. Dips, drinks, fermented finger food, toppings, sauces and soup. Your menu will be as unique as you are.

Being surprised is part of the fun!

Clear off your biggest table or garden bench. Grab some flowers from the yard or grocery store and shove them randomly into a jar for the table. Spread out a cotton cloth to absorb the drips and spills that are sure to come.

Pile some plates and cups and napkins and forks at one end. Nestle some bottles of probiotic drinks into an ice chest at the other. As friends arrive, find a place at the table for their casseroles, baskets and bowls. Offer them a cup of goodness and a plate of appreciation.

On this occasion, your table is a picture of love. The meal is a time for gratitude. Make a toast to the life that burbles inside each person in attendance. And say a prayer of thanks for the random feast you've set together.

It's a social table of sustenance. It's a community table of cooperation in supporting one another physically, spiritually, and socially. Your potluck table is an expression of identity that is both unique and mutual in the culture we share.

L'chaim – to life!

APPENDIX

Tools you might need to get started

If you're anything like me, you probably don't want to make a huge investment in something you're not sure you'll even like doing or eating. Fortunately, the basic items you need to get started are easy to find.

Not all of the equipment listed in this book is crucial for fermenting success.

For instance, you don't NEED a canning funnel, but it helps get your chopped fruits and veggies into your jars without spilling a lot.

You don't NEED an airlock lid. You can just "burp" regular lids to release gasses as they accumulate.

You don't NEED an Instant Pot or yogurt maker. You can create a warm spot for fermenting and culturing foods in any number of ways.

Fermenting on a shoestring

If fermenting were an expensive endeavor, people like me would never get a chance to try it. But our ancestors were fermenting for many generations throughout history without pricey tools.

For instance, my great-grandmother kept her ferments in recycled bottles and crocks in what was supposed to one day become "the bathroom" in their family home. It was a small, unplumbed extravagance built onto the house, which was situated near the railroad track in Weatherford, Oklahoma. She never did get an indoor bathroom, but instead had a great fermentation chamber.

Below is a list of items I've mentioned throughout these pages and where you may be able to get them. I'm sure that you already have many of these items. Others are easy to pick up by shopping online, at local stores or at garage sales in your neighborhood. I have had great luck at thrift stores. Don't discount the idea that a neighbor may be more than willing to share what they have.

Note of warning: Fermenting can be addicting.
Proceed with caution!

TOOLS	INGREDIENTS	CULTURES:
Find tools online, in thrift shops, hardware stores and retail stores	Find ingredients at Farmers' markets and Grocery stores	Find cultures online, at Yemoos.com, kombuchakamp.com, floridasunkefir.com or a friendly neighbor
Glass jars (wide mouth) various sizes Swing top bottles Lids Cloth covers or paper coffee filter Sauerkraut pounder Bowls Sharp knife Yogurt dripper Yogurt maker Instant Pot Non-metal Sieve Wooden Spoon Measuring cups Measuring spoons Grater Zester Food processor or Blender Canning funnel Weights Followers Electronic scale Dehydrator Thermometer Pitcher Glass (Chalk) marking pens Stick blender Food grade plastic squirt bottle Juicer	Non iodized salt Organic sugar, brown and white Miso Paste Liquid whey Fruit juice Fruit Vegetables Tea Non-chlorinated water Spices Herbs Wine and Spirits	Milk kefir grains Water kefir grains Kombucha SCOBY

A Closing Note

Time for a testimony…

Adding fermented foods to your daily diet can precipitate a major change in your gut health over time. It changes your energy level. Boosts your ability to fight infection. Even your mental health can be affected by what you eat.

Most of my diets through life have been about losing weight. Not so much about gaining health.

When I hit a certain age, the weight wanted to creep up and up. And nothing helped, short of just not eating. Gotta say that starving myself proved to be very un-vitalizing. I got sick all the time. I felt like #*&% all the time. My brain was not working all the time. Joints hurt. Back hurt. Allergies blossomed. And some unmentionables happened, too.

Then came the idea to ferment.

Chopping, smashing, sloshing, salting and waiting. Then eating.

Uh-oh, bad reaction to histamines.

Histamine is a natural compound occurring in fermented foods. Histamine isn't usually a problem for people. A healthy gut is full of enzymes that break down histamines. But if your gut isn't healthy yet, eating and drinking foods with histamine can cause allergic reactions.

I stepped away from eating the fermented foods for a little more than a month. Then I restarted slowly. Just a taste. Then a little more the next day. If everything went well I had a little more.

(Too much information?)

Bit by bit, my innards were changing. Every now and then my body seemed to want to suddenly empty itself of something or other, so I just let it happen. Then things got better. Then a month or so later, another purge took place naturally. I got to thinking that maybe that was a good thing.

One day it hit me that it had been a long time since I had caught a cold. I was laughing a whole lot more than I used to. Although I've never been one to exercise, I began to take long walks nearly every day, enjoyed it, and came home feeling stronger.

After almost a year of making and eating fermented foods, I ran into an old friend who mentioned how well I looked – she said I had "good color." That's the "glow" of eating fermented foods that you may have heard about. She did not mention that I was slim and trim, because I was not. Eating fermented foods hasn't been a weight loss journey for me. Too bad about that.

But I feel as if I'm on the road to stronger immunity, less inflammation and higher energy level – both physical and mental.

Here's to you:

It's my greatest wish that you will discover your own journey to better eating and greater health through fermented foods.

Be patient. Notice small victories. Connect, relate, share… and party every night. You've got the time. You've got all the rest of your life – which I hope is filled with many delicious years to come.

Made in the USA
Middletown, DE
14 August 2021